RUSSIA AND THE KYOTO PROTOCOL

The Energy, Environment and Development Programme (formerly the Sustainable Development Programme) at Chatham House seeks to advance the international debate on energy, environment and development policy and to influence and enable decision-makers – governments, NGOs and business – to take well-informed decisions that contribute to achieving sustainable development. Independent of any actor or ideology, the Programme does this by carrying out innovative research on major policy challenges, bringing together diverse perspectives and constituencies, and injecting new ideas into the international arena. The Programme's core financial support is provided by generous contributions from:

- Amerada Hess
- Anglo American
- British Nuclear Fuels plc
- BG Group
- BP plc
- Department for Environment, Food and Rural Affairs (UK)
- Department for International Development (UK)
- Department of Trade and Industry (UK)
- ExxonMobil
- Foreign and Commonwealth Office (UK)
- General Direction for Energy and Mineral Resources, Ministry of Economy, Finance and Industry (France)
- Saudi Petroleum Overseas Ltd
- Shell International
- Tokyo Electric Power Co. Inc.

Mike Bartlett

KING CHARLES III

NICK HERN BOOKS
London
www.nickhernbooks.co.uk

A Nick Hern Book

King Charles III first published in Great Britain in 2014 as a paperback original by Nick Hern Books Limited, The Glasshouse, 49a Goldhawk Road, London W12 8QP

Reprinted in this revised edition in 2014

King Charles III copyright © 2014 Mike Bartlett

Mike Bartlett has asserted his right to be identified as the author of this work

Cover image by NBstudio.co.uk

Designed and typeset by Nick Hern Books, London
Printed in Great Britain by CPI Group (UK) Ltd

A CIP catalogue record for this book is available from the British Library

ISBN 978 1 84842 441 8

King Charles III was first performed at the Almeida Theatre, London, on 3 April 2014 and transferred to the Wyndham's Theatre, London, on 2 September 2014. The cast was as follows:

CHARLES	Tim Pigott-Smith
SARAH/GHOST/ TELEVISION PRODUCER	Katie Brayben
WILLIAM	Oliver Chris
HARRY	Richard Goulding
SPENCER/NICK/SIR GORDON	Nyasha Hatendi
MR EVANS	Adam James
CAMILLA	Margot Leicester
COOTSY/CLIVE/SIR MICHAEL	Tom Robertson
MR STEVENS	Nicholas Rowe
JAMES REISS	Nick Sampson
JESS	Tafline Steen
KATE	Lydia Wilson
MUSICIANS	Belinda Sykes, Anna-Helena McLean

From 8 September there was the following cast change:

JAMES REISS	Miles Richardson

Director	Rupert Goold
Designer	Tom Scutt
Composer	Jocelyn Pook
Lighting Designer	Jon Clark
Sound Designer	Paul Arditti
Casting Director	Joyce Nettles
Associate Director	Whitney Mosery
Movement Director	Anna Morrissey
Musical Director	Belinda Sykes
Associate Lighting Designer	Peter Harrison
Associate Sound Designer	Christopher Reid
Assistant Director	Jessica Edwards
Voice and Text Coach	Alison Bomber

Sonia Friedman Productions, Stuart Thompson Productions and Almeida Theatre, in association with Lee Dean and Charles Diamond and Tulchin Bartner Productions present the Almeida Theatre production.

Thanks

Thanks to Tom Dingle and the Jersey Arts Trust, Jonny Donahoe, Rupert Goold, James Grieve, Headlong, Robert Icke, Clare Lizzimore, George Perrin, Ben Power and Tom Scutt.

M.B.

For Samuel

Characters

KING CHARLES III
CAMILLA, DUCHESS OF CORNWALL
WILLIAM, DUKE OF CAMBRIDGE
CATHERINE (KATE), DUCHESS OF CAMBRIDGE
PRINCE HENRY OF WALES (HARRY)
JAMES REISS
MR EVANS, *Prime Minister*
SPENCER
COOTSY
JESS
MR STEVENS, *Leader of the Opposition*
GHOST
SARAH
NICK
CLIVE
SERVANT
PAUL
SPEAKER OF THE HOUSE
FREE-NEWSPAPER WOMAN
TERRY
SIR GORDON
BUTLER
SIR MICHAEL
TELEVISION PRODUCER
ARCHBISHOP OF CANTERBURY

And CLUBBERS, ATTENDANTS, MEMBERS OF
PARLIAMENT, COMMUTERS, PROTESTERS, MEMBERS
OF THE PRESS

Note on Text

(–) means the next line interrupts.

(…) at the end of a speech means it trails off. On its own it indicates a pressure, expectation or desire to speak.

A line with no full stop at the end indicates that the next speech follows on immediately.

Prologue

A choir sings.

The funeral procession of Queen Elizabeth II goes past.

ACT ONE

1.1

Enter CAMILLA, *Duchess of Cornwall, and* KING
CHARLES III.

CAMILLA.
   My wond'rous Charles you looked composed throughout
   You did her proud, for as she would have liked
   You never showed your pain, but stood instead
   A virtuous man of dignity and grace.
   Immovable, inscrutable as stone.

CHARLES.
   Please don't. It's simply what I had to do.
   We'll find no dignity in cov'ring up
   The way we feel. What son should, standing
   Waiting at his mother's grave, stop his tears?

CAMILLA.
   Are you alright?

CHARLES.
   My whole existence has like most of us
   Been built upon the ones who gave me birth.
   And now they're gone. That's it. First Dad. Now Mum.
   The only truth: I am alone.

CAMILLA.
                         Except for me.

CHARLES.
   It's not the same, Camilla. The love, with us,
   It's all my life, but never can replace
   Parental word, a mother's hand to hold.
   But here – the others – back to statue –
   It's Catherine, and William.

   Enter WILLIAM, DUKE OF CAMBRIDGE *and*
   CATHERINE, DUCHESS OF CAMBRIDGE.

Hello! You're radiant, despite the grave
Restrictions of the mourning dress. It is
Your gift my dear, it's what you've brought to us.
A sense of fashion, better hair as well.

KATE.
I never thought I'd see her pass away

CHARLES.
I felt the same.

WILLIAM.
How are you Dad?

CHARLES.
…

WILLIAM.
It must be hard to deal with loss combined
With gain. For soon, at last, you will be King

CAMILLA.
Not soon.

WILLIAM.
Three months –

CAMILLA.
Your father rules today.

KATE.
I thought the coronation marked the change

CHARLES.
You're right, officially that is the case –

CAMILLA.
But England, Scotland, Northern Ireland
They cannot stand without a king or queen
For all the months it takes to organise
A coronation –

WILLIAM.
Wales.

CAMILLA.
Wales what?

WILLIAM.

                                        Wales too.

You missed it out.

CAMILLA.

Then Wales. As well. And Wales!

KATE.

But surely constitutionally speaking –

CAMILLA.

Oh sweet my dear we have no constitution
Instead Tradition holds us to account.

KATE.

Tradition then, it still –

CAMILLA.

Tradition holds that on the death of kings
Or queens, the next is monarch straight away.
He needs no proclamation, needs no man
To shout 'The Queen is dead, long live the King'.
Your father ruled the moment Granny passed.

KATE.

So coronation day itself is just
The ancient costumes worn, and lines to learn,
A slice of theatre, that's played for fun?

CHARLES.

Not fun I think, for me, I hate those things.

HARRY *enters*.

CAMILLA.

Harry! It's such a joy to have you home.
Even in such morbid circumstance as this.

HARRY.

I might head off. If that's okay? I know there's this thing,
but I'm tired.

CHARLES.

You want to go? Of course, we'll say you're ill, if that's –

HARRY.

Yeah right, that's it, I don't feel well. Yeah.

CAMILLA.
Why? What's the matter?

HARRY.
Er… Headache? But that was all good wasn't it? It went okay, from what I could see?

KATE.
Do you really have to go?

HARRY.
It's not… I mean… the whole… I've only been back a few days, can't deal with all the chat. The people. It's such a change from being out there.

CHARLES.
It's important Harry.

HARRY.
Yeah but the headache though.

They look at each other for a moment.

Then he goes.

WILLIAM.
We should leave, and mingle with the crowds.
A single round should be sufficient, then
We're at the Palace, yes?

CAMILLA.
                    That's right.

CHARLES.
                              But where's
The children?

KATE.
                    Taken now to Kensington.
They needed sleep.

CHARLES.
                    They didn't cry.

WILLIAM.
                              They – what?

CHARLES.
> I thought they would. With both of them so young.
> But something in them understood and so
> They watched and listened, and like all of us
> They kept their real emotions to themselves.
> In public William, you were the same,
> For as a babe so silent in the cot
> We worried you might quietly have died.

WILLIAM.
> We felt the same with George. The first-born brings
> A paranoia.

CHARLES.
>   True. The constant fear
> That one might somehow lose one's son.

Enter JAMES REISS, *his Press Secretary, who waits.*

WILLIAM.
> But Dad, you're shaken up.
> Perhaps we should take time to talk?

CHARLES.
> I'm sorry. It must wait. James wants us now –

CAMILLA.
> Charles – James will happ'ly do whatever you
> Command. You can spend time with William –

CHARLES.
> We'll see you later on.

A pause.

WILLIAM.
> Alright.

They go.

JAMES.
> Just Mr Evans, waiting now, to speak.
> Before you walk together from the door.
> I am afraid the press are kettled up
> And staying all this time, expect their shot.

CHARLES.
A moment please, alone, before it starts.

JAMES *goes*.

Camilla you as well, I'm sorry but...
You understand?

CAMILLA.
I do.

She kisses him, and goes.

CHARLES.
At last. I needed room for thought to breathe
In every second since my mother passed
I'm trapped by meetings, all these people ask
Me questions, talking, fussing, what to do,
Expect I'll have opinion there, all good
To go, like Findus ready meals for one,
Pre-wrapped and frozen, 'This is what I think.'
As if I know! My better thoughts – they start
From scratch, slow cooked, and brewed with time.

My life has been a ling'ring for the throne.
Sometimes I do confess I 'magined if
My mother hap'd to die before her time,
A helicopter crash, a rare disease
So at an early age I'd be in charge –
Before me years of constant stable rule.
But mostly I have hoped she'd keep in health
That since for most, outrageous dreams and hopes
Are all they'll ever have, and yet their life is full,
So I am better Thoughtful Prince than King.
Potential holds appeal since in its castle walls
One is protected from the awful shame
Of failure.

JAMES *enters*.

JAMES.
Your Majesty, the Prime Minister's here.

CHARLES.
Bring him in.

JAMES *goes*.

No more, exactly as Camilla said,
Although the crown has yet to sit upon
My head and burden me with gold,
I am the King default, and will ascend.

MR EVANS, *the Prime Minister, enters*.

MR EVANS.
Your Majesty.

CHARLES.
Prime Minister.

MR EVANS.
Sincere condolences upon your loss.

CHARLES.
A loss I think that all her subjects share.

MR EVANS.
Of course, we miss our Queen. But you will feel
A sharper pain, I'm sure.

Pause.

You felt she would have liked the service?

CHARLES.
I trust she would, for planned it was by her.

Pause.

MR EVANS.
I hope you heard the people outside cheer?

CHARLES.
When? No. A cheer? A cheer for what?

MR EVANS.
Towards the end from through the doors and walls
We heard hip-hip and all at once there came
Hooray, and then three times repeated same.
And, although perhaps the tone was wrong
At least it showed they cared and loved the Queen.

CHARLES.
I didn't hear, my mind must have been somewhere else.

JAMES *enters*.

JAMES.
Your Majesty. Mr Evans. The press await.

CHARLES.
We'll talk some more across the weeks to come.

MR EVANS.
We will indeed.

Pause.

CHARLES.
But now you must excuse me, for I have
To walk from here, and face the baying mob.

JAMES.
Your Majesty you may not recall we did
Decide for public reassurance you
Would leave with Mr Evans at your side,
The Crown and State, Prime Minister and King.

CHARLES.
We did agree?

JAMES.
                    Indeed.

CHARLES.
                              You're right.

JAMES.
                                        Just so.

CHARLES.
You're right I don't recall. And now we're here
I feel instead I should remain aloft
From politics and walk with royals alone.
I'm sure Prime Minister will understand

MR EVANS.
Of course, I'll go right now, and clear the way.

JAMES *and* MR EVANS *go*.

CHARLES.
Such equal billing was a joy when Prince.
To share the stage did spread attention out.
But now I'll rise to how things have to be
The Queen is dead, long live the King. That's me.

CHARLES *goes*.

1.2

HARRY *and* SPENCER, *in the VIP room at Boujis*.

Behind them, out in the club itself, CLUBBERS *mill about with drinks – dancing*.

SPENCER.
Look, I completely understand you must respect a serious period of mourning and all that boohoo, but you deserve a classic night out, and here's something to cheer you up. Recommendation from my father. Import from Eastern Europe.

SPENCER *produces a black bottle*.

It's black. That's all we know.

SPENCER *takes the top off and* HARRY *swigs some. It's strong and disgusting*. COOTSY *enters – wearing jeans and a cheap top*.

COOTSY.
Hello bitches. Wagwan.

SPENCER.
Speak English Coots.

HARRY.
What's all that?

COOTSY.
Don't know what you mean?

SPENCER.
You look like you got raped by Primark.

COOTSY.
Undercover mate.

SPENCER.
What?

COOTSY.
Student night in New Cross. Couldn't go in what I usually
wear, they wouldn't know what hit them. Ergo: dress down.

HARRY.
Why were you at a student night?

COOTSY.
To get your surprise.

HARRY.
Coots –

COOTSY.
She's a lovely girl. Very distinctive. Asked her if she wanted
to meet you, she was keen. I've brought her back. Now
you're out the army thought you might want to, you know –

HARRY.
Coots.

COOTSY.
Do a pleb.

HARRY.
Yeah.

COOTSY.
Knob a prole.

HARRY.
Not in the mood.

COOTSY.
Approach a subject from a different angle.

HARRY.
Where is she?

COOTSY.
Toilet. Making herself look presentable. Best she can. Her name's Jess.

SPENCER.
What's she like?

COOTSY.
Don't know, mate. Can't get past the voice.

JESS *enters. She's mid-twenties, well dressed, clearly clever.*

JESS.
Er… hello.

COOTSY.
Jessica!

JESS.
Not joking then.

COOTSY.
What?

JESS.
Here he is. Prince Harry.

HARRY.
Yeah?

JESS.
Is Charles really your dad?

HARRY.
What?

JESS.
Or was it the other one?

SPENCER.
The other one?

JESS.
Yeah. What's his name?

SPENCER.
No.

JESS.

Hewlitt.

SPENCER.

Hewitt.

JESS.

Her butler or whatever.

SPENCER.

Not the butler.

COOTSY.

No the butler didn't do it.

JESS.

Cos you're very ginger. I don't think that's a bad thing, but if
you haven't done a test yet you should, cos if Hewlitt was
your dad instead, you'd be out of the family.

HARRY.

What?

JESS.

Free of it!

HARRY.

Why would I want to be free of it?

JESS.

Cos you hate it. Don't you?

Beat.

HARRY.

…no.

SPENCER.

He really doesn't.

JESS.

Yeah you do. He *does*, this dressing up, getting wrecked, it's
because you're part of this big thing, but you don't get
anything back. You'll just be the drunken uncle, get married
a few times, always pissed. A trap. For you. Isn't it?

HARRY.

That's what you think?

JESS.
Yeah.

HARRY.
So what should I do then?

JESS.
What?

HARRY.
What should I do instead?

JESS.
You really want to know?

Beat.

COOTSY.
Look, I think it's time for you to tap out darling. Go on. Off
you pop. We've seen girls like you before, won't be long
before the cameraphone comes out –

HARRY.
Cootsy, Spencer, someone wants you at the bar.

COOTSY.
You telling us to leave, mate?

HARRY.
Yes I am.

COOTSY.
Er – You realise she's probably a Socialist or something?

SPENCER.
No. Alright. Come on. Not wanted.

COOTSY.
Harry, word of warning, she's just a bit of fun yeah? That's
all she's supposed to be. Pop and stop yeah? Drive-through.

They go. Now it's just JESS and HARRY.

JESS.
Your mates are idiots.

HARRY.
They're loyal.

JESS.

There's something a bit sweet about you, isn't there?

HARRY.

That's what people say.

JESS.

You come across really badly on TV but in person you're... shy.

HARRY.

So, are you going to answer my question?

JESS.

What should you do instead? Come on.

HARRY.

Where are we going?

JESS.

Prince Harry.

You have no idea.

1.3

MR EVANS *enters with* CHARLES.

Tea is on the table.

A pause.

CHARLES.

Shall I be mother?

MR EVANS.

Thank you, yes, that's kind.

CHARLES *pours the tea.*

CHARLES.

Well good, so how shall we begin?

MR EVANS.

Well oft I run through current legislation
Or international matters sometimes might

Take precedence, but here today I thought
We might commence by talking of a bill
About to land upon your desk that seeks
The royal approval.

CHARLES.

                    Yes? What bill d'you mean?

MR EVANS.
To limit future growth and mass expanse
Of runways. What environmental checks
There are, have long been out of date –

CHARLES.

                                        You must
Excuse me, much as this wants our attention,
I had assumed we'd start with something else.

MR EVANS.
Of course. Whichever subject you would like.

CHARLES.
Your bill concerning privacy, that sets
Restriction on the freedom of the press.
I understand it's passed the House and soon
Will be the British law, is that correct?

MR EVANS.
That is correct, the regulation of the press
We feel is overdue, and although we would
Prefer them in an ideal world to keep their house
In order by themselves, this has been tried,
So many times and each time failed.

CHARLES.
I've read the bill.

MR EVANS.

                    You have? Well, good.

CHARLES.

    …

MR EVANS.
What else is there to say, the bill has wide
Support across the House both Commons and

The Lords, and will today arrive with you
For signature to enter into law.

CHARLES.
You like this bill?

MR EVANS.
I absolutely do.
For we have seen, and you yourself must know
Too well the lasting wounds the press inflict.

CHARLES.
…

MR EVANS.
We cannot risk another murder case
Where phones belonging to the dead are hacked.
It cannot be a right or civilised
Country, in which, in any private place
A toilet, bedroom, might be there concealed
A tiny camera, then these photos 'splayed
As front-page news, the consequences thrown
Around the world and everlasting, so
Without a jury, judge, or evidence
A punishment is meted out, a life
Is ruined, reputation murdered.

CHARLES.
You do not think a principle is here
At stake, that something vital to our sense
Of freedom, both as individuals
And country whole, is being risked?

MR EVANS.
Your Majesty.
Of course I understand that view and have
Myself considered where the balance lay.
But both within the House of Commons and
In every poll conducted 'cross the land,
There is opinion something must be done.
The law is what your people want –

CHARLES.
They want

The leaders they elected standing up
And making choices they themselves cannot,
Because they have not time, they pay their taxes well
So we, or you, may take the time to study hard
And make the right decision on the day.

MR EVANS.
I know, I have, and this is what we think.
I have to say it does surprise, that with
The great intrusion they have made into
Your life, you'd have them left untouched like this.
What of the pack of wolves that mercilessly
Did hunt to death your late and much-missed wife

CHARLES.
That's bold. So soon in our relationship.

MR EVANS.
What's bold?

CHARLES.
                    To utilise Diana.

Beat.

MR EVANS.
I'm sorry, but in fact it's rare to have
To justify the passing of a law like this.
I would have thought of all the victims
You'd feel the strongest something must be done.

CHARLES.
As a man, a father, husband, yes I do.
But that's not who we are when sat with you
In here, not just am I defender of
The faith but in addition I protect
This country's unique force and way of life.
We are not strong for manufacturing
Politically our sway and influence
Are in decline. But still we demonstrate
The way a just society should work:
Judiciary, democracy and more –
A low corruption rate. All those who hold
The strings held to account themselves in turn.

MR EVANS.
 Your Majesty, thanks, I understand and say
 I will, if opportunity transpires,
 Make sure I take your view into account.
 Perhaps we should move on to other things.

CHARLES.
 It is the law on privacy that holds
 Concern. And so I ask you tell me what
 As my Prime Minister you do intend.

MR EVANS.
 The law is made, and passed. It is too late.

CHARLES.
 My views to you mean nothing then

MR EVANS.
 Your views mean much, but on this subject yes.
 I disagree with what you think and if
 You want my true intent, I will say more:
 That even if there was a chance to change
 The bill to take account of what you think.
 I would not see it done. The public vote
 To choose the members of their Parliament
 And that is where decisions will be made
 Not in this room between the two of us.
 But sir, now please, it matters not, because
 The law is drawn, and voted on and passed.

CHARLES.
 Then our weekly meeting's done.

 Pause.

MR EVANS.

                                        Your Majesty –

CHARLES.
 And thank you Mr Evans, though we don't
 Agree it has been most informative.

MR EVANS.
 I do apologise if I have caused
 Offence, I simply wanted to explain my view.

CHARLES.
And so you have, we'll meet next week.

CHARLES presses the buzzer.

If you could send him in.

MR EVANS.
                    Then I should leave.

CHARLES.
I think you'll know my next appointment well

Enter MR STEVENS, *the Leader of the Opposition.*

Ah Mr Stevens. Here, you recognise
My guest.

MR STEVENS.
                    I'd not expected Mr Evans –

CHARLES.
I reasoned thus: In case there did arise
An accusation that my vision here
Of left and right was being tilted out
Of proper balance, only meeting one.
I will from now make sure each week I have
The usual half an hour with my good
Prime Minister, but then give equal time
For Leader of the Opposition too.

Pause.

How does this sound?

Pause.

MR EVANS.
Your mother never felt the need, but if
It is your wish, then good, you must.
But I should leave so you can gather up
Opposing views from that I've tried to give.

He goes.

MR STEVENS.
Forgive me sir, but I am rather shocked
By sarcasm I would have thought did not

Have place in royal conversation such
As this. He seemed to be, well, quite annoyed.

CHARLES.
He is a man of principle. I hope he will
In time see how a conversation 'tween
The two of us cannot threaten him,
But merely gives perspective.
For instance he believes we need this bill
To safeguard privacy, I'm not so sure.
Your party voted 'gainst it, am I right?

MR STEVENS.
We did, indeed. We felt as writ it was
Restrictive to our freedom of the press.

CHARLES.
And this, your vote, was no way influenced
By other factors: need for good PR,
Donations to your cause, or party funds...

MR STEVENS.
That's not –

CHARLES.
I have it with authority
You are good friends with editors and have,
On numerous 'ccasions had them round to tea.

MR STEVENS.
The cut and thrust of public life, you know

CHARLES.
The briefing paper that I had, it said
At Christmas Eve you gifted one of them
A horse.

MR STEVENS.
Now look. That's lies. Not true.
It was a pony for her daughter, who
When our two families met at lunch one day,
Expressed a want for such a beast and so
When thinking what to get them come Noel –

CHARLES.
Despite all that, your group of friends is not
Why you were keen to stop the current law.
Instead it was on principle.

MR STEVENS.

Correct.

I do not think it right.

Pause.

CHARLES.
It is too late. And so the first law passed
As King will be a law that's dangerous.
I always hoped as Crown I'd have some small
But crucial influence upon the State
I'd given all my working life to serve.
But Mr Evans does not like me, and
Has made explicit that he will not change
A single thing in light of what I say.
And if this is the case then what am I?
My mother gained respect from what she'd seen.
The Blitz, she sat with Churchill, and met all
The most important figures of her years.
But what am I?

MR STEVENS.
It may not be too late to stop the law.

CHARLES.
But Houses Parliament and Lords have cast
Their votes and therefore when I sign the bill –

MR STEVENS.
If you sign the bill.
For surely that requirement remains
Your choice, that is the power you possess.

CHARLES.
A ceremonial right, not one to use.

MR STEVENS.
I hate to differ but I think this strikes
The heart of why we have a queen, or king.
They are the check and balance of our land.

I've long believed that we could never see
A Nazi Party making British laws
Because the reigning monarch then would stand
His ground and being Head of State refuse
To sign, refuse to let the country lose
Democracy, and doing so, provoke
Revolt. Perhaps I am romantic but,
I think the signature holds something more.

CHARLES.
It's not our place, would do more harm than good.

MR STEVENS.
Then not important, write your name in ink,
And unamended let it into law.

CHARLES.
Thank you Mr Stevens.

MR STEVENS.
Your Majesty.

MR STEVENS *goes*.

CHARLES.
I hoped that once in place, an instinct here,
That had been dormant up till now would thrive,
And override my indecisive mind
But now I'm Majesty, and feel the same.
A weakling shadow of what went before –

Enter GHOST.

But wait! What's that? I need to get some sleep.
I thought I saw a shimm'ring light, just in
The corner of my eye, a floating thing –

Mother?

Exit GHOST.

She's gone, and now she has, I'm not quite sure
If she was there at all, perhaps it was the light –
I'm certain all she was, was nerves and ills.
I'll call my doctor now for sleeping pills.

Exit CHARLES.

ACT TWO

2.1

No. 10 Downing Street.

MR EVANS *and* SARAH, *his Chief Political Adviser, enter.*
SARAH *is reading the bill.*

SARAH.
　　It's just a joke, we shouldn't waste the time.

MR EVANS.
　　When last we spoke he seemed disturbed about
　　The passing of this bill.

SARAH.
　　　　　　　　　What do you mean?

MR EVANS.
　　I mean he didn't want it law at all –

　　NICK, *his Communications Adviser, enters, with* CLIVE.

NICK.
　　Prime Minister, the underbutler's here.

MR EVANS.
　　And Stevens?

NICK.
　　　　　　　On his way.

MR EVANS.
　　　　　　　　　　　You said to him
　　Emergency?

NICK.
　　　　　　I did indeed.

MR EVANS.
　　　　　　　　　　As soon
　　As he arrives, you send him in.

NICK.

                      Of course.

NICK goes. MR EVANS *turns to* CLIVE.

MR EVANS.
    Right then, hello, I'm Tristan, what's your name?

CLIVE.
    It's Clive, your honour.

MR EVANS.
                    Clive, relax, and now,
    In detail tell me 'bout this letter brought.

CLIVE.
    This morning at eleven, when I would
    On normal days bring coffee – right – the King
    Did turn and give to me the envelope
    You have there now, and said I should
    Without delay deliver it myself
    To Downing Street. I said that perhaps
    He might be better sticking to his own
    Long-tested postal system? i.e. Royal Mail?
    But he was firm and so not wanting to
    Arouse the regal ire early in
    A promising career I donned my coat
    And through the rain approached the gates where there,
    Surrounded by a crowd of tourists all
    With cameraphones, I said my piece that was
    The truth to the policemen standing wait.
    And not replying really all they did was laugh.
    At which point I displayed the seal in wax
    Upon the letter and I said it bound
    The papers tight, as their armorial crest
    Upon their helmet bound them to their King.
    Their laughter stopped, they checked the seal, and then
    Did finally 'llow me entrance, and I'm pleased
    To see you with the letter safely home.

    Beat.

MR EVANS.
    You did not see the contents then?

CLIVE.

                     When I
Did hand the letter to your servant here
The seal was quite intact. I haven't read a word.

SARAH.

Well thank you Clive, I think that's all we need.
You may go back to Buckingham Palace.
And continue with your underbutlering.

CLIVE.

Thank you both. I will.

He goes.

SARAH.

You're shitting me. Is this a fucking dream?
It seems you are correct, our King is mad,
And taken to communicate with us
In methods from the nineteenth century.

MR EVANS.

It is a point. He wants us all, but mostly me,
To think again upon this bill and then,
Resend, or not.

SARAH.

                     If word got out, that he
Within a month of sitting on the throne –

MR EVANS.

Before he has. The coronation's not
For some time yet.

SARAH.

                     Right so, before he's e'en
Throned or got a crown to call his own
He's chosen to exert this power that
His wiser mother never thought to use.

MR EVANS.

I always hoped that he above the rest
Possessed a mind to understand the world.

SARAH.

You hate the royals, Tristan you always have.

MR EVANS.
    I hated what they stood for, yes, but hoped
    That with a King who wanted progress –

    NICK *enters*.

NICK.
    Mr Stevens sir –

    MR STEVENS *enters*.

MR EVANS.
    It's good to see you Mark. And thanks you came
    So soon.

MR STEVENS.
            Well I was told emergency –

MR EVANS.
    Please have a look at this, it came today.

    MR STEVENS *looks at the letter.*

    Of course, all that we say inside this room
    Is confidential, kept between ourselves.

MR STEVENS.
    Of course.

    He reads.

    I see, and have you spoken to the King?

MR EVANS.
    Not yet, I thought it better if we were
    As head of both the largest parties met
    In full agreement what response we give.
    Assuming, as we must, we leave aside
    The matter of the bill and look instead
    At simply what His Majesty intends.

MR STEVENS.
    You know I didn't like this bill at all?

MR EVANS.
    I do, but as I say it's not the point.

So in the conference you had did he
Give any hint he might differ like this?

MR STEVENS.
We had a range of conversations that,
On touching many subjects, may have glanced
The privacy law. But as you know, it must
Remain discreet between the King and I.

MR EVANS.
Of course, but did he say –

MR STEVENS.
                                        I left him as
I found him, sure that he would sign the bill.

MR EVANS.
And now he has refused, what is your stance?

MR STEVENS.
In fact I do agree. We cannot have
The King approving laws depending on
His own opinion, or the way he feels.
Well, what do you intend to do, so that
We may, without distress, or publically
Embarrassing our newly minted King
Explain to him the simple duty that
He must uphold, whatever his own mind.

MR EVANS.
I thought that as he said he liked a range
Of views, from both sides of the House, we might
Together go and there persuade him.

MR STEVENS.
Although appreciating any hand
Outstretched across the aisle, I do believe
In such a constitutional issue as,
This surely is, it is important that
While choirs carry passion but the words
Are lost in many voices sung at once,
So we in politics must all step back
And in agreement believing in just one,
Entrust our finest soloist to sing.

You are, unlike myself, elected sole
And only leader of the British Isles.
I am convinced the message will sound best
And most authoritative said by you.

MR EVANS.
And if, once done, he still won't sign I'd have
Your full support in standing by the bill?

MR STEVENS.
Of course. We are conservative in more
Than party name. Tradition has its place
And here it does protect our right to vote.
His Majesty must not object. That's clear.

MR EVANS.
Good then, I'll try to see the King today.

MR STEVENS.
That sounds, to me, a plan, Prime Minister,
It is uncharted waters we're thrust towards
But thank you for consulting me in thought
In this, be sure, you have my full support.

He goes.

2.2

Buckingham Palace.

HARRY *enters. He's with* JESS.

HARRY.
Leicester Square! Quiz machines, Tube platforms –

JESS.
What's this then? Your gallery?

HARRY.
'Wetherspoon's', 'Wagamama', they're full, just full of
people – And your best idea – Dans le Noir! A restaurant
where you eat in the pitch darkness. They thought I was an

estate agent. We talked about mortgages! Then your flat, with a boiler that doesn't work, and no carpet, but everything is yours. You can do what you want, TV, Doritos, curry – I want more, Jess. More of all of that.

JESS.

No one's stopping you.

HARRY.

A night, yes, but I can't do this with my life –

JESS.

Why not?

HARRY.

It's not what I was born into –

JESS.

Then change it. Look at all of this – it's absurd it still exists. The world you were born into… It's paid for by those people in Wagamama, you take money from their hard work and you spend it on portraits, palaces, and in your case flights to Las Vegas. It's not your money to spend.

HARRY.

You're very beautiful.

JESS.

Don't patronise me – listen to what I'm saying.

HARRY.

I am, I know what you're saying and I agree with it, I'm just also saying that you're beautiful as well.

JESS.

Er – calm down. My mates you met last night want nothing less than the abolition of the monarchy.

HARRY.

Yes I know.

JESS.

They also said under no circumstance was I to get off with you.

HARRY.
   Don't then.

JESS.
   Don't worry. I won't. It's been a great night. Hope you've
   had something to think about. I'll… see you.

   Beat.

HARRY.
   It's just you really look like you want to kiss me.

JESS.
   Yeah, but I don't.

   They get closer.

   They kiss.

   Enter JAMES.

JAMES.
   Oh! Excuse me, Your Highness. I'm interrupting.

HARRY.
   What? No. This is James Carbury Reiss

JAMES.
   Cadbury –

HARRY.
   Cadbury Reiss, the Press Adviser for the Palace. He's
   worked for my father for twenty

JAMES.
   Thirty

HARRY.
   Thirty years. I know him really well. This is Jessica.

JAMES.
   Pleased to meet you. How do you know the Prince?

JESS.
   We met in a club.

JAMES.
   Lovely.

HARRY.

Yeah, we haven't been to sleep since two days ago – James, we went to Sainsbury's. You know what Sainsbury's is?

JAMES.

I do.

HARRY.

It was the middle of the night and we just shopped for stuff. I got a Scotch egg.

JAMES.

I see. Were your security present to ensure there was no footage taken?

HARRY.

James it's not like that –

JAMES.

Miss Jessica, may I ask what you do for a living?

JESS.

Student.

JAMES.

Of.

JESS.

Art.

JAMES.

Art.

JESS.

Yes, I'm currently exploring Islam's relationship to pornography.

JAMES.

Oh dear. Harry, how well do you know the young lady?

HARRY.

Really well. We've talked all night, about everything, she's brilliant.

JAMES.

What's her surname?

HARRY.
     What?… Her name's Jess.

JAMES.
     Jess what?

Beat.

     Highness. Your grandmother the Queen for nearly seventy
     years has recently passed away. The country's in a position
     that very few people have ever experienced before. This is
     perhaps the most unstable moment the Royal Family will face.

HARRY.
     So?

JAMES.
     So… perhaps a conversation should be had about timing.

HARRY.
     …

JESS.
     What does that mean?

JAMES.
     Your Highness.

He goes.

JESS.
     Right. That. That there. Is why I'm not getting off with you.
     I've had enough, see you later Harry.

HARRY.
     No wait. Stay. I… I want you to stay.

JESS.
     Why?

She turns to leave, but WILLIAM *enters with* KATE.

HARRY.
     Oh –

JESS.
     What?

HARRY.

My brother and his wife – please. Just… Be nice.

They make to go the other way but WILLIAM *calls to them.*

WILLIAM.

Ah Harry, there you are! They said you'd been
Discovered parading round the Palace grounds

HARRY.

And now we're leaving thanks a lot, goodbye.

KATE.

But wait, we haven't met, always the same
With Harry, must be in his training some
Efficiency of drill or army thought
Means he forgets his manners. Hi. I'm Kate.
And this my husband William –

HARRY.

                              No wait –
She doesn't understand, she's deaf and dumb.
Not dumb, that much, a bit, she speaks sometimes
But chooses when, unfortunately now
Is such a moment she can't talk. And since
She's deaf as well, she didn't hear a word
You said, that's why she isn't smiling much,
And looking at me in that funny way.
We really should be going though, before –

JESS.

Yeah okay hi. Of course I know who you are. Wow. 'William
and Kate.' Jesus.

WILLIAM.

This is unusual.

HARRY.

I'm just showing her the Palace –

KATE.

Are you from Reading?

JESS.

Er… yeah. Why?

KATE.

>Heard the accent. Me too! Well not – like it was a village nearby.

JESS.

>I'm from Purley.

KATE.

>Purley! We used to go there sometimes and hang out on the weir.

JESS.

>We did that too. Smoked a bit of weed. Didn't know you were from there.

KATE.

>Fuck yeah!

HARRY.

>Okay. We're going to bed.

WILLIAM.

>Okay.

HARRY.

>I mean separately. Separate beds.

WILLIAM.

>I'm not really interested. Good to meet you Jess.

JESS.

>You too. 'William'… Weirdest. Day. Ever.

>HARRY *and* JESS *go*.

KATE.

>Perhaps just as you hoped he's growing up
>She's quite unlike his normal horsey girls
>This Jess I liked, she's rather down to earth.
>But what's the matter husband, since we sat
>And had expansive breakfast, while our King
>Did talk, you seem distract and pensive-like.

WILLIAM.

>When offered what he's wanted for so long
>I thought Dad'd seize the moment, and renewed,
>Go greet the people, smiling, talking with

The press to so ensure the public know
The man who is about to hold the crown.
Instead by all accounts and what I've seen
He stays inside, just reading books, and bills
It isn't what I hoped.

MR EVANS *enters.*

MR EVANS.
Oh Lord, good William and Kate, they said
I was to wait, and soon the King would join.
They didn't mention you were settled here
As well. I'll quickly go and sit elsewhere.

KATE.
Mr Evans, stay a moment, please, we just
Were taking time to look upon the walls

MR EVANS.
The walls, Duchess?

KATE.
Indeed, for there in paint
And brush, the very best of kings and queens
From days ago. Together they narrate
A story of succession, of a change.

MR EVANS.
Yes. Indeed. It is a time of change, that's true.

KATE.
But sir – you look so pale, distraught, you must
Sit down, we'd rather that, than have you faint.

MR EVANS.
You're kind to me.

KATE.
So sudden, what's the cause?

MR EVANS.
You will forgive me if I do not give
The detail of my conference, it is
A matter of some delicacy.

KATE.
But if it causes such distress –

WILLIAM.

       Of course.
We understand and will not press on you.
Perhaps some water?

MR EVANS.

     Thanks. Again, you're both so kind.

WILLIAM *exits through the door.*

KATE.

This must be something virulent indeed
That does affect the King as strongly as
Prime Minister. For William himself,
Did just a minute hence, remark he thought
That Charles seemed quite as out of sorts as you.
Perhaps it is an illness passing round?

MR EVANS.

No illness, Duchess no, a matter that
Need only trouble him and I, for now...

KATE.

For now?

MR EVANS.

    Why yes, because if forced,
It could, in time, cause problems for us all.

KATE.

Please tell me what. Perhaps I might
Relieve the harshness of this mystery sore.

A beat. MR EVANS *shows her the bill.*

MR EVANS.

In reading here, you mustn't tell a soul,
What's written or not written by the King.

She reads. WILLIAM *enters with a glass of water.*

WILLIAM.

Here Mr Evans, water, fetched and got
By careful hand of Prince of Wales.
But Kate what on that paper makes
That look? Which from experience I know

Tends doom and fury from your normally soft
And poised face. You seem distressed. Here –

KATE.
Yes, read. I take it this is not a fake.

MR EVANS.
Brought by butler, phone call did confirm
The fact that Charles has marked it there himself.
And I as people's leader come to say
This will not stand, he must allow the bill
To pass both signed and unamended.

KATE.
But William, why would your father decide
To interfere so crassly in affairs of State?
My husband, what say you?

WILLIAM.
                                    Nothing.

KATE.
                                            Say what?
Say more. For nothing comes of nothing said.

WILLIAM.
My father's King. He may have reason that
We do not know, or understand as yet.
Our loyalty lies to serve the wishes of
His Majesty, and here in ink is writ
His want in black and white. So that is that.

KATE.
But Mr Evans!

WILLIAM.
                        Stands his ground as right
He must in representing those whose votes
Empower him to lead. But we as son
And daughter of the Crown will only give
Support, and leave dispute to those who have
A stake in what is being argued on.

KATE.
You have a stake. Much more than most.

Enter CHARLES.

CHARLES.
So here you are, all met. We've Kate, my son
Prime Minister as well. I surely hope
The Prince of Wales and Duchess welcomed you
And made you comfortable. Well, have they? Yes?

MR EVANS.
They have Your Majesty. For when thirsty I
Did mention water, Prince of Wales did then
Go fetch it thus himself, and bring it hence.

CHARLES.
A future king waits butler-like upon
The people! That awaits us all, perhaps.

WILLIAM.
We will depart, allowing you to talk.

KATE.
Goodbye Your Majesty, and Prime Minister,
We'll see you soon, I'm sure, we will.

They go.

CHARLES.
Well Mr Evans here you are, and there,
You hold the way I feel about your law.

MR EVANS.
Firstly, it is my fault that when we met
I failed to help you understand the way
The voice of monarch has effect. It is –

CHARLES.
You're patronising now, that's worse, at least
Before you made assumption that I knew
The role of Crown, but now you name me fool.

MR EVANS.
No sir, it's not what I intend at all
But how can I progress with such an act?
You hope I'll take it back to Parliament?

CHARLES.
>You take it back, you say that there is fault
>In how the bill is drafted, say you've thought
>Again. The House does then once more debate
>And having done, whatever come of that
>I will accept and sign, without delay.

MR EVANS.
>But with respect, you've not authority
>To refuse our will like this, you're not elect.

CHARLES.
>I worry that, in time to come, this will,
>Have greater consequence than you
>Or I can tell, that maybe –

MR EVANS.
>Forgive me sir to interrupt, it's not
>The content here discussed, but just the fact
>You will not sign. The Opposition too,
>With me agree that even though they did
>Not want the bill, and would not have it law –

CHARLES.
>You've talked to Mr Stevens?
>What said he?

MR EVANS.
>The same. That you must sign.

A beat.

CHARLES.
>But yes, of course he said I must.

MR EVANS.
>Your Majesty, have you thought what people will
>When hearing that you have reserved assent,
>Be wont to do?

Pause.

>If word of any part of this did reach
>Outside these walls, division would result.

I beg you sir, let's talk some more as months
And years go on, but here it is. Perhaps
You can just get your pen and sign the bill.

CHARLES.
You have not changed a word?

MR EVANS.
It is the same.

A pause.

Were there solution evident that could
Enable both of us to have our way
I'd take it in an instant for I know
You're acting out of conscience.

CHARLES.
That's right, and in good conscience I have thought
That come the moment, surely I could sign.
But when the pen approaches paper thus,
About to store for ever my assent
And tell the future generations that
King Charles did let this happen, and, in proof
Applied the value of his name beneath,
The pen dries up, my hand it cannot write.
For if my name is given through routine
And not because it represents my view
Then soon I'll have no name, and nameless I
Have not myself, and having not myself,
Possess not mouth nor tongue nor brain, instead
I am an empty vessel, waiting for
Instruction, soulless and uncorporate,
And like I saw on television when
I was a younger man, I'm Charles no more
The human being, but transformed into
A *Spitting Image* puppet, lying prone
Upon the table waiting for some man
To come and then inserting his own hand,
Do operate the image of the King
Pretending life, a simulation of
The outer skin with nothing in the heart.

MR EVANS.
This is your role, you surely must have known –

CHARLES.
But I'm not sure if ever in the past,
That there was such a bill, that changed the way
That speech is granted freedom. Not since
The news was born, has Government and State
Been there allowed to use the threat of jail
To stop the presses, based on what they deem
Is unacceptable. The Queen did not
In all her years bethroned, face laws like this
To pass.

MR EVANS.
                    I do agree for in her time
She faced far greater revolution when
She lost an Empire, granted that the law
On homosexuality be changed
She oversaw the alteration from
The unions, mines and factories that stood
For generations to a world
That, Thatcherated, Reaganised, did place
The profit higher value than the pride
Belonging to the man who travels day
By day upon the Clapham omnibus.
And through all this, when laws arrived from those
Prime Ministers she hated, doing things
Of which I'm sure she never would approve.
She still did sign, respected all the votes
Empowering those elect to make the law
She always signed. She always gave assent.

CHARLES.
Well I cannot.

MR EVANS.
                    And I in turn cannot
As British leader stand to let this go.
I'm sorry sir, but if I leave this room
Without King Charles imprinted here below,
I cannot keep it secret and will tell

The world that simply you refuse to sign.
And in addition I'll ensure this bill
Becomes the law without your royal assent.

CHARLES.
Your first assurance, making public what,
Their newly risen King has failed to do
Is your prerogative, so go ahead,
But second that you can pass laws yourself
Without consulting Head of State is wrong.
My lawyers are agreed. You may not like
My medicine but you cannot legally
Dispute its high authority.
Redraft the law with changes that defend
The independence of the press and send
It back and I will sign immediately.

MR EVANS.
Your Majesty, no.

Pause.

You're sure that this is what you want to do?

CHARLES.
Without my voice, and spirit, I am dust,
This is not what I want, but what I must.

MR EVANS *goes.*

ACT THREE

3.1.

MR EVANS *addresses the people outside No. 10 Downing Street.*

MR EVANS.
With the bill concerning privacy
And statutory regulation of
The press, the King has unexpectedly
Refused to grant assent, on grounds that he
Does not concur with what it does intend.
I have done all I can, to ease his mind.
But he is not persuaded, and despite
His certain knowledge that the royal assent
Is ceremonial, and not a tool,
He has continued to withhold his pen.
We're currently negotiating still
In order to progress, but here I say
Importantly, that first we must defend
Democracy itself, and leave aside
Our diverse views on what the bill contains.
So to this end, I will here make a pledge
That either printed with the royal assent
Or standing firm without his regal sign
The measure will be law within the month.

3.2

CHARLES *speaks from Buckingham Palace, to the people, on television.*

CHARLES.
I'm speaking from the Palace to you all,
Reluctantly, tonight. I had a hope
My ministers and I could find a way
To circumvent a public feud like this.
But driven by my conscience, I have declined to pass
A law that would give Government the right
And power to restrict, and then decide
What is acceptable to say in print.
Once fragile politicians can,
While claiming public sensitivity,
Go censoring what's writ or not, it will
Be easier to govern as corrupt
Than bother being held unto account.
And therefore I, who stands outside the rough
And tumble of expedience,
Do caution them, and ask they think again.
So far, they have refused, so now do I,
As King, and servant to the populace,
Request your understanding, and your trust,
That this, a rare but necessary act
Is not me stepping too far from the throne,
But is my duty and fulfilling what
The King or Queen is sworn by oath to do.

3.3

Evening. Quiet.

JAMES *waits, impatiently. Enter* JESS.

JAMES.

Miss Edwards. Here at last. Well better late
Than not at all, although I don't yet know
Your wish so maybe that's not true.

JESS.

Yeah okay.
I need to speak, but Harry can't know

JAMES.

And here it is.

JESS.

Here's what?

JAMES.

The trouble that
From years of managing these things I sensed
Was brewing from the moment that we met.

JESS.

I know you don't approve of me.

JAMES.

How true.
But I'm late home so tell me what you want.

JESS.

Increasingly there's stories in the news
About the Prince and I. They think I'm an
Unusual match for him, and so explore
My past and present, calling up my friends

JAMES.

This is to be expected I'm afraid.
There's really nothing to be done.

JESS.

I know and just so long as it's about
My politics I'm actually fine with it.
But there's a buried story that they will

Uncover and would cause embarrassment
Not just to me, but to the Prince.

JAMES.

                              I see.
It's for this reason I preferred the Prince
Did stick to Sloanish fluff. But now it seems
He fancies you instead, so yes, what's wrong?

JESS.

Three years ago, when I was only young
And starting out, I knew a boy called Fin
Who was a dick if truth be told. But we,
Because we lived in different cities then
Did text our love, instead of meeting up.

JAMES.

Oh dear.

JESS.

          That's right

JAMES.

                    I'm guessing where this goes.

JESS.

One day, when I was in the mood I had
Composed a text expressing love and such,
Which I then sent to him. But now he does
Make contact once again, and threaten me.

JAMES.

He threatens you with one small text –

JESS.

                                  Yeah well –
In truth it did contain additional form.
A token of my love

JAMES.

          A token, right –

JESS.

And although I'm not the kind of girl
Who plays around like that, I must confess
I took a picture that… well… it was private.

JAMES.

I really don't need the details –

JESS.

But he last week, made contact and did say
He'd seen the news and since I wanted gold,
He should have his. He threatened then to send
The photo to the *Sun on Sunday* if
I do not pay him cash.

JAMES.

Well that's a shame.
But as I said there's little I can do.
It's blackmail so you could approach police.
But they, I warn you leak like carrier bags.
And have no love for matters royal these days.

JESS.

Come on, if this was Harry or the King you'd do something –

JAMES.

With respect, you're not part of the family.
If truly miss you wish to save the Prince
Perhaps you need to leave his side, and doing so
Take from this man the power he now has.

Enter CHARLES.

Have you thus far met the King?

JESS.

Not yet. Oh God.

JAMES.

Then can I suggest that this is not the time.
Go now –

JESS *and* JAMES *leave, not seen by* CHARLES.

CHARLES.

Opinion polls suggest that people are
Divided almost equally as to
If my non-signing is within my rights.
Or not. But that half's far more than I
Expected would agree with me on this.
Whatever many like to think, there is

A wise and ancient bond between the Crown
And population of this pleasant isle.
It's only in the last five hundred years
That politicians and democracy
Have led the way in policy and meant
The people vote for who they want to lead.
And this is right, but unlike countries which
Did build existence through the parliament
This is to us, an option added on,
Like satnav on a car, it does not come
As standard, and the car will function well
Without, it drives, protects, it normally goes.
And though it's wise to pay for extra help,
And usually the voice of the machine
Assists us well to get from A to B,
When lost, and crisis strikes, we soon mistrust
These modern ways, and reach for what we know:
We seek the map, from years before, and there
Do stabilise and resecure our way.

CAMILLA *enters*.

CAMILLA.
I stupidly had thought that once you're King
Perhaps it would reduce the angst you feel.
Instead your face has lines I never saw before
And in this light your hair looks far more pale
Than I remember. Is it worth the pain?

CHARLES.
I don't know if you're right. I do avoid
The mirror in the last few weeks it's true,
But in myself I feel much greater strength.

CAMILLA.
You sit there at your desk and work and read
Which means we cancel trips that should be made
And let down crowds who have looked forward to
Your presence there.

CHARLES.
                    It is these days, when I
Define my monarch's voice. I need the time.

CAMILLA.
> But that's not what the people want.
> Remember that the fulsome praise the Queen
> Did most receive was that she always filled
> Her duties even in the latest years.
> And similar for you, remember when
> In Somerset the Levels sank beneath
> The waters of the flood, you were the first
> To wade into the problem and were met
> With clapping, admiration, and despite
> The upset there, so many smiles! For you
> Their future King had given hope where hope
> Had disappeared. And now they need the same.
>
> *Pause.*
>
> Dear Charles, I wasn't sure to tell you, but
> Someone waits to see you here tonight.
> I know it's late, and when I heard he had
> Arrived so unannounced I said to hold
> And let you finish dinner, then we'd see
> Your mood, before we grant him audience.

CHARLES.
> Not Mr Evans? No, I'm tired, tell him –

CAMILLA.

>   It's
> Mr Stevens waits.
>
> *A moment.*

CHARLES.
> Send him in, and leave us here to speak.

CAMILLA.
> Be careful Charles, I do not trust him well.
>
> *She goes.*
>
> *Enter* MR STEVENS.

MR STEVENS.
> Your Majesty, please forgive how late it is
> I was not keen to draw attention to
> The fact we have a conference tonight.

CHARLES.

> I'm sure you're not, since vocally you've been
> Most critical of what I've done, despite
> A week before, within this very room,
> Assuring me of your complete support.

MR STEVENS.

> Forgive me but I never offered that.
> Support in private, yes, but all I did
> Was draw attention to your rights as King.

CHARLES.

> A politician's tongue you have indeed
> And weasel mouth.
> It's late. I've had enough. Cut to the chase.

MR STEVENS.

> Perhaps you know that Mr Evans will
> In two days' time bring forth a bill within
> The House that makes it clear a law cannot
> Be halted waiting for the King's assent.

CHARLES.

> …

MR STEVENS.

> This bill is sure to pass. And subsequent
> The bill of privacy. And from then on
> Not only this particular law but all
> The legislation still to come, will not
> Appear before the monarch's eye, or pen.
> You will not only fail upon this one
> And only thing, but in fact, the Crown
> Will lose the right to speak forever more.
> So I had wondered what Your Majesty
> Did plan to fix this far erroneous course?

CHARLES.

> …

MR STEVENS.

> Because, you see, you only have two days.
> And I for one would not be happy that
> The influence our monarch has, is changed.

CHARLES.

Therefore you think the better evil is
Take pen, and sign the wretched and corrupted bill?

MR STEVENS.

I would be sad that it would come to that.

CHARLES.

What then?
You speak as if you have a good idea.

Beat.

MR STEVENS.

Well this is why I'm not officially here
It means I can say words to you that I
Will not have said –

CHARLES.

                    …the politician's tongue.

MR STEVENS.

But now you see it has its purposes.
It is not up to me, to tell the King
What he has privilege to do, but if
He needed inspiration he could mull
How William the Fourth resolved a not
Entirely different situation.

Beat.

CHARLES.

You speak in circles. Now say what you mean.

MR STEVENS.

Your Majesty no, because I am not here.
I just suggest you might research the past.

But it is late, so I should go and rest.
I have a tingling that the next few days
Will one way or another bring disrupt
Tempestuous waking sleeps unto us all.

MR STEVENS *goes.*

CHARLES.

The stakes are raised again, and now I feel

Unease, I know well the precedent
Of William the Fourth.

A draught blows.

It's cold tonight, I should insist they fix
This draught that late at night blows tempests through.

Enter GHOST.

But no – not now, again, it is the same
Beshrouded lady, walking through the walls
You are not real! It cannot be! Go! Now!

GHOST.
My darling Charles your face it is so pale
You often looked in thought, but not like this

CHARLES.
It said my name.

GHOST.
You think I didn't love you that's not true
I always cared I always wanted best
But you rejected me, and so away
I went.

CHARLES.
Diana...?

GHOST.
But in all that time
I never hoped, I never thought that you –

CHARLES.
What do you mean, you never thought –

GHOST.
Never reckoned on the fact that you as Crown
Who worries 'bout the way you look, and stroke
Your hair down into place, and nervously
Do touch above your lip when getting sad.
Will be the greatest King we ever have.

CHARLES.
The greatest King?
But stop, please wait! I didn't understand!

Explain!
But no, it drifts away, like mist at dawn.
Oh God, if anyone did see me now
Their brand-new King, who, sleepless runs towards
The made-up nonsense in his head, but yet...
She is quite beautiful, I know the walk.

The GHOST *goes.*

'The greatest King', what did that mean?
My mother ruled for seventy years, she must
Be counted straight away a greater Crown.
Unless implied the ghost a single deed
That's done or not. A punctuation that,
Making stronger impact hitting once
Does with surprising shock and awe achieve
What slow experience could not.
Perhaps there's wisdom in insomnia
And sleep does drive me where, awake, I fear.
In sense, I fold and pay the heavy debt.
But madness says to play, and up the bet!

Exit CHARLES.

3.4

Night. WILLIAM *enters in his pyjamas.*

WILLIAM.
    It is a strange and ambulous night
    I lay flat out but then there was a noise,
    That woke me in a second, high it was
    A scream I thought, the kind that I have heard
    When women inconsolable and full
    Of tears do try to breathe. But not for years,
    Since I remember through the door and walls
    Of my lost mother's bedroom we could hear
    Her cry herself to sleep at night, have I
    Encountered such a shriek as that.

Enter HARRY.

You're never up this early in the morn
Unless for you it's still the night before

HARRY.
I'm sure I heard a scream.

WILLIAM.
                              And so did I

HARRY.
So like our mother's voice it freaked me out.

WILLIAM.
I've checked and there is nothing going on.

HARRY.
Well that's the story of my life.

Beat.

Once woke I lay and thought I've had enough.
You will be King, and Kate your Queen.
And even if our father's making waves
At least he is allowed to choose his course
But I am doomed for ever just to chase
Your wake, a ginger joke, bereft of value.

WILLIAM.
The way our father acts the joke may be
On all of us.

HARRY.
                    But then I turned to speak
To Jess, who slept tonight with me, and found
That she had gone, and in her place a note.
Which read she thought that it would never work.
She would embarrass me, she said.

WILLIAM.
                              I thought your Jessica
Did cheer your mood, the two of you had fun –

HARRY.
We have, she DOES. And not just fun. We have
Done things that most do every day, but I
Assumed were not within my compass

Royal, she has unblinkered me, and op'd
My eyes. The world is wider now, more depth
And shape, but with this new perspective I
Do only seem more trapped, more narrowed down
By this, the family. I thought she might
Be glowing exit from this regal hole
And 'scape me from a life of humorous
Periphery, but now, upset, she's gone.

Pause.

WILLIAM.

It is a passing mood. There will be girls
To come, there always have before, but if
Our father's crisis black does shadow more
I hope that I can turn, as I have always done,
To you, and you'll be there, already at
My side, the pact our mother made us make
As resolute as on the day was sworn.

HARRY.

What was the scream?

WILLIAM.

                    I do not know.

Beat.

HARRY.

Here's Kate, she'll make me worse, I'll go
And find a greasy spoon, and maybe when
I'm back our father will have blown this all
To kingdom come and I'll be free at last.

He goes. Enter KATE.

KATE.

What is it husband troubles you like this?

WILLIAM.

The trouble that you had me countenance
So long ago, but which I did ignore.
You're right of course, my father's waited for
Too many years to call the crown his own.
And now he overestimates its worth,

And makes it ruler over King himself.
So Gollum-like he, craven, fears to sign
This bill, in case the precious crown shouts 'Weakling,
    traitor King.'

KATE.

And therefore you must go persuade at once
Your father of the damage he inflicts.

WILLIAM.

You know I cannot make the case myself.
For since Mum died he's wondered if myself
And Harry are more loyal to mother lost
Than to our father who survived and aged.
To question him on such a subject, when he
I know, will be embattled and besieged
Will in a second make him draw away
Instead, I have called forth Prime Minister.

KATE.

You mean he'll be here in the morning light?

WILLIAM.

Why no I called for him at once tonight.

SERVANT *enters*.

SERVANT.

Your Highness Mr Evans waits outside.

KATE.

Well right on cue, he's punctual as well.

WILLIAM.

Go back to bed, and leave all this to me.

KATE.

I will not go, for surely you'll be King
Some day, but on that day I am as much
The Queen, and I do not intend to be
A silent partner in that regal match.
Please show him in!

SERVANT.

                I will Duchess.

He goes.

WILLIAM.
Before, when sleeping, did you hear a scream?

KATE.
What scream?

WILLIAM.
               A high and terrifying sound.

KATE.
I didn't hear a thing. A scream? Who screamed?

MR EVANS *enters.*

Good Mr Evans what a kindness shown
To rise from bed at early hour thus.
I fear my family does cause you pains.

MR EVANS.
My lady I cannot pretend that, yes,
My life would be a joy in recent weeks
If Britain was republic.

WILLIAM.
I've heard that you intend to call together
The members of the House and then propose
Exclusion of the Crown from making law.

MR EVANS.
Tomorrow, yes.

KATE.
               Tomorrow? What? So soon?

MR EVANS.
Ideally I'd preserve our current mode.
But as things are I haven't got a choice.

WILLIAM.
Will you consider waiting for a week
And giving time to let my father change?

MR EVANS.
Already we have waited, and he changes not.

KATE.
>But what if William went at earliest hour
>To see his father and persuaded him.

WILLIAM.
>No Kate, I can't. That's not –

KATE.
>What time's the vote?

MR EVANS.
>   It's twelve o'clock.

WILLIAM.
>My Catherine I did make it clear I'll not
>Inflict the same division on ourselves
>That currently does tear at our country.
>Instead I wondered if Prime Minister
>Might have one more attempt. I cannot think
>That if my father truly understood –

MR EVANS.
>He comprehends it well. He will not sign.
>I have no choice.

KATE.
>   My nervous future King!
>You must go now and tell him what to do.
>Because it's not just him, or you, you risk,
>By sitting here and doing nothing thus,
>It is our children, and their children hence
>And after that all generations royal
>That are to come in future years, they all,
>Do look to you insisting you defend
>The Crown against this fool's indulgence.
>I say this not as future Queen but just
>As British woman proud of both my State
>And King, with understanding that it is
>A balance in a contradiction
>'Tween those elected and those born to rule
>That is unique and does protect and make us all.

WILLIAM.
>It wouldn't change a thing. He is too proud.

KATE.

> Then think not only of persuading him
> But finding lever so he must agree.

WILLIAM.

> What lever?

KATE.

> Say the thing that must be said.
> The fact that both of us command support
> That does near thrice outweigh the aged King
> And if we wanted might begin to itch
> In waiting for the throne.

WILLIAM.

> You stop right now.

MR EVANS.

> I think perhaps that I will leave you both.

KATE.

> I say what you two gentlemen will not.
> There is another way to solve this thing.

WILLIAM.

> That is the opposite of all that I believe.
> I'll never step across my father's right.

KATE.

> In that case Mr Evans, fare thee well.
> Good luck tomorrow casting off the last
> Remains of ancient and outdated royals.

MR EVANS.

> I'm sorry it has come to this. I really am.

MR EVANS *goes*.

WILLIAM.

> You did embarrass him.

KATE.

> He's fine and laughs at us as we decline.
> My husband look at me! My love for you
> Is full and as the moment that we met.
> I do not think you weak at all but *wrong*.
> Become the man I know you are and act.

WILLIAM.
I am not King.

She looks at him, then goes.

My wife knows not that in the years before
My grandmother did pass away,
She sat with me for hours at a time
And because I made a point to ask,
Did talk to me about what she had learned.
She told me that temptation lies as royal
To act, and speak, and lead, and always move,
When actually the greatest influence
That we can wield is through our standing still
Not rash, and never changing, a great Crown
Is made by dint of always being there,
I'll keep my silence. And let life unfold.

A noise.

But what was that? Perhaps it's Kate come back?

Another noise.

But not from her direction, maybe something –

The GHOST *appears.*

Oh God, a glimmering and hov'ring form

GHOST.
Oh William!

WILLIAM.
She cries my name, I know
That voice.

GHOST.
Oh William, you're now the man
I never lived to see, so tall, and proud.

WILLIAM.
Mum?

The GHOST *touches his face.*

He cries.

GHOST.

But still the face remains the same, and there
The eyes hold kindness, yes, but suffering too.
Such pain my son, such hurt, but now be glad.
You'll be the greatest King we ever had.

WILLIAM.

Don't go!

The GHOST *leaves.*

This comes of waking wrongly in the night.
Perhaps some sleep will fix the problems that
Awake I cannot solve. So I'll to bed.
But still... The greatest King? That's what she said.

He goes.

3.5

A kebab van.

HARRY, *exhausted, goes up to it.*

There's no one there. He bangs on the side.

PAUL *appears – he's bright, upbeat.*

PAUL.

Yeah mate?

HARRY.

A kebab please.

PAUL.

Ooo. Too late. Switched it off.

HARRY.

Please... I'll pay more.

PAUL.

...Okay okay. Doner?

HARRY.

Yeah.

PAUL *starts serving the kebab.*

PAUL.
Long night?

HARRY.
I... I think I might quit my job.

PAUL.
Ah – be careful about that. Way things are, I mean we all have shit jobs, don't we? Maybe it's different for you. You sound a bit posh, don't want to be rude but perhaps your mum and dad can help you out or something –

HARRY.
My mum's dead.

PAUL.
Oh right. Mine too. I suppose everybody's mother dies one day.

HARRY.
Yes.

PAUL.
Even the King. His mother dies, he doesn't cry, what's that about?

Why do you want to quit then?

HARRY.
I think I'm in love.

PAUL.
Pretty girl?

HARRY.
Yeah.

PAUL.
You want to run off with her? Start a new life.

HARRY.
Maybe.

PAUL.
Just warming up – that's four eighty.

HARRY *pays with a five-pound note*. PAUL *looks at it*.

Out of date now innit?

HARRY.
Suppose so.

PAUL *starts to cut the kebab meat*.

PAUL.
You know since she died. World's gone mad. I swear. Every
night, people have this look. Bit like you – They come here,
they want a kebab, a Coke, and it's like they're terrified. And
I think I know why. They don't know where they live. They
don't know what Britain is any more.

HARRY.
What do you mean?

PAUL.
Slice by slice, Britain's less and less. You cut the army, that's
one bit gone, squeeze the NHS, the Post Office closed, the
pubs shut. Devolution. Less and less. Smaller all the time
and when does Britain get so cut down, that it's not Britain
any more?

HARRY.
You think that's now?

PAUL.
Well the Queen's dead. If you take enough layers away, what
have you got left, underneath, know what I mean? Maybe
she was what held it together.

HARRY.
I've got no layers left.

PAUL.
What? Here you are.

He gives him the kebab.

Where's this girl of yours then?

HARRY.
She left me.

PAUL.
  You love her.

HARRY.
  I… yeah. I think I do.

PAUL.
  That's something then. Find her. Night.

  PAUL *shuts up the van again.* HARRY *eats the kebab,*
  walking off –

3.6

The House of Commons.

MEMBERS *enter on both sides of the House.*

MR EVANS *and* MR STEVENS *face each other across the*
despatch box.

The SPEAKER OF THE HOUSE *rises.*

SPEAKER.
  Order!

  Order!

  This House will come to order now! At once!
  We here discuss a move to raise ourselves
  Out from the overseeing shadow that
  For centuries has held us to account
  And so it's not the moment to become
  A bunch of children, stamping up and down.
  Both major party leaders now will speak.
  And then we'll vote at once and there forthwith
  If passed, by special measures made, the bill
  Will straight go to the House of Lords who wait
  Upon us even now to take this vote.
  So first the Leader of the Opposition.

MR STEVENS.
  I thank you Mr Speaker and because

We know the facts upon the matter well.
I will unusually be very brief.

Shouts.

Our Parliament exists to make sure that
The people of our country do decide
The codes and principles by which they live.
It is a contract made between a man
Or woman, and the State, by which both sides
Must there agree, that citizen does have
A voice and in return will keep the law.
And so an intervention in this way
That so removes the voice, but keeps the law
Is absolutely wrong, and in this House
Must every vote support this vital bill.

He sits. Cheers.

SPEAKER.
The Prime Minister!

MR EVANS.
I make assumption that we all will vote
In favour of this bill, for we all here now
Have made a choice to come and represent
Constituents to have their say in this
Their House, and give their weight and 'fluence to
The shaping of the government and law.
Although we have the Crown as Head of State
Both history and precedent do hold
Him in his place. And now he oversteps
So we must act and not impertinent
Or rude, or out of disrespect but since
We have no other choice than to protect
Our democratic, British, way of life.

Cheers. He sits.

SPEAKER.
And now by ancient process, we divide the House and –

Three knocks.

We will divide the House to vote, ayes to the –

Another three knocks.

Please will someone, before we vote, go see
What causes this infernal knocking there!

Another knock.

CHARLES *walks in, without a crown, but regally dressed,
and with the sceptre.*

The MEMBERS OF PARLIAMENT *stand.*

CHARLES *stands opposite the* SPEAKER.

CHARLES.
Empowered by ancient decree I do,
As King of England, Northern Ireland, Wales
And Scotland, use my royal prerogative
To here dissolve the Parliament at once.

A pause.

Shouting from the MEMBERS.

SPEAKER.
Order! Order! I will have silence now!

The shouting dies down.

CHARLES.
This noise demeans you all. Is this the space
Where public will is spoke and heard, or just
A stand for juvenile and selfish squall?
Through petty theft, and fighting here amongst
Yourselves, you've lost the population's trust.
I am not prone to certainty but you
Have drawn that measure in my unsure heart.
Unlike you all, I'm born and raised to rule.
I do not choose, but like an Albion oak
I'm sown in British soil, and grown not for
Myself but reared with single purpose meant.
Whilst you have small constituency support
Which gusts and falls, as does the wind
My cells and organs constitute this land
Devoted to entire populace
Of now, of then, and all those still to come.

And in their interest, in their voice
The Speaker knows it is within my right,
To sack my ministers and call a fresh
Election.

Shouting of the House.

SPEAKER.
Order! Order! Gentlemen! Please!

The shouting continues.

CHARLES *takes his sceptre and bangs it hard on the floor.*

Silence.

CHARLES.
My Speaker, will you here confirm to them
That what I do is well within my right
And anointed power to, as King, demand?

A pause.

SPEAKER.
Your Majesty…

                              …if this is what you want.
Then this, you can, as King, command.

Shouting. CHARLES *turns and goes.*

Interval.

ACT FOUR

4.1

The sound of a protest throughout the scene.

Enter FREE-NEWSPAPER WOMAN, *handing out papers to passing* COMMUTERS, PROTESTERS, *etc., throughout.*

FREE-NEWSPAPER WOMAN.
Free *Standard*. Free *Standard*!
In times like this a paper feels absurd.
Unless we could reprint the articles
In every second, news contained in here
Is counted history. When King does march
And Parliament is forcibly dissolved
When Labour leader says we should remove
The King, and Tory says he isn't sure.
It's changing every second and my point of view
Is make him sign somehow and then we're done.
But I'm alone. Most people are enraged.
They march at day, and then at night they camp
Outside the Palace, shout against the King.

A MONARCHIST PROTESTER *– wearing country gear – tweed, and a flatcap, enters. She has a placard – 'God Save the King'. She has a bloody nose and is panicked – running away – looking round. Terrified.*

Although there's only a few thousand now,
The numbers grow. And sometimes there's a brave
Supporter of the King who tries to take
Them on and this has sparked some violence –

A roar of the crowd and a group of ANTI-MONARCHIST PROTESTERS *storm the stage. The* MONARCHIST *panics, throws the banner to the ground and runs away. The* ANTI-MONARCHISTS *head off, in pursuit.*

Another ANTI-MONARCHIST *watches them go. He's wearing a 'V for Vendetta' mask, carrying a banner: Charles with a Hitler moustache. A slogan 'Charles Out'. He takes out a pre-rolled fag, puts it in his mouth without taking off the mask. A moment to himself.*

But none of this is on page one.
Because in truth it's not much fun.
It takes up two to twenty-five
But visually the public's eye
They know will drift to this instead
A photo of a girl in bed.

The protester takes off the mask, and we see it's JESS.

Wait – do I know you?

JESS.
　　Don't think so –

FREE-NEWSPAPER WOMAN.
　　Yeah… wait…

She looks at the front page of her paper. Compares it. A few PROTESTERS *walk past and stand in a circle.*

Hang on – I do!

HARRY *enters.*

HARRY.
　　Hi.

JESS.
　　Oh… Oh come on! You can't be here. You might be lynched, on your own.

HARRY.
　　I'm not on my own.

JESS.
　　What?

HARRY.
　　Terry?

One of the 'protesters' turns to HARRY – *lifts up his woollen hat.*

TERRY.
Yes sir?

HARRY.
Everything under control.

TERRY.
Yes sir. For now.

TERRY *pulls his hat back down, undercover.*

HARRY.
That's how I found you. I know why you left. I saw the story. It's okay.

JESS.
Harry. None of my friends are talking to me. Every second people recognise me and laugh. And I never wanted any of it. I don't want to be famous and I don't want anything to do with that. Or you. Not any more.

HARRY.
You mean that?

JESS.
Yeah. Just… go home.

HARRY.
But I don't… I don't know what to do without you.

JESS.
You'll be okay.

HARRY.
There must be a way.

JESS.
No mate. You're a prince. And you always will be.

She picks up her banner. A growing chant from the crowd.
TERRY *turns to* HARRY.

TERRY.
Sir we should be moving.

HARRY.

Jess… I've got an idea. Come with me. Back to the Palace.

JESS.

No.

HARRY.

One last chance.

Please.

Give me an hour.

The crowd getting louder.

JESS.

It won't work.

HARRY.

It might.

JESS.

I'm a Republican.

HARRY.

I know. But you're beautiful.

The crowd scream.

Please.

JESS *relents and goes with* HARRY. TERRY *follows.*

The sound of the crowd gets louder and louder.

4.2

Buckingham Palace.

The sound of the crowd outside.

Enter SIR GORDON – *Chief of the Defence Staff, and*
CHARLES.

CHARLES.
Sir Gordon, thanks indeed for coming here
At such short notice, would you like a drink?

SIR GORDON.
Your Majesty, I am refreshed, and keen
To hear how I can be of use.

CHARLES.
                    The crowds
Outside. You hear? It's every day.

SIR GORDON.
                       I know.

CHARLES.
They're passionate, and from what I can tell
Extremely keen for my untimely death.

SIR GORDON.
They're unemployed and students, all they want
Is good excuse to make some noise, it's fine.

CHARLES.
I am reminded of that day, the year
It was that I was married to Diana.
And on the Trooping of the Colour when
The Queen was leading, riding out in front
And trotting down the Mall in glorious sunshine
There came from somewhere in the crowd six shots,
Aimed at my mother, echoing around.
The horse was panicked and reared up at once
In contrast to the ever-steady Queen,
Who calmed the beast and simply carried on,
While round her much too late, the guards did run
And startled like the horse, did throw themselves

Into the crowd, to find the armed man.
Of course we learnt he fired blanks that day
And merely wanted fame. But now I think,
It's likely when, in time, those shots are aimed
At me, I'll only get to hear the first.

SIR GORDON.

It's natural sir that you will be concerned
When constantly this rabble rave and shout.
But rest assured you are protected well.

CHARLES.

How many guards are standing there outside?

SIR GORDON.

Because you are in residence, we have
At all times four, in front, and then of course
There is the royal police within the walls,
And extra agents that protect yourself.

CHARLES.

It is the guards in front that bother me.
Please have them tripled, at all times I want
Twelve men to there be visible to all.

SIR GORDON.

Your Majesty, these men in front are there
For tourist ceremony, not defence.
If it's your safety that concerns, may I –

CHARLES.

It is my preservation and I know
That will be served by what the public see.
The truth is that my greatest enemies
Stand not within the crowd outside but there
In Whitehall, waiting for the slightest glimpse
Of weakness.

SIR GORDON.

                    So... I see. You want a show of strength.

CHARLES.

Sir Gordon, these are, in truth, strange days.
And so, when timely pressed, you'll need to know

Precisely where, to whom your loyalty lies.
If Government, of course, I'd understand.
But possibly you think, like me, that King
Can on occasion ask the Parliament
To reconsider what they mean to do.
For that is all I ask. To think again.
Sir Gordon, in the end it's up to you.

Beat.

SIR GORDON.
My loyalty?

Beat.

Perhaps I can suggest Your Majesty
That in these times of severely heightened threat
It would be wise not only to increase
The armed guard that stand outside the gate
From four to twenty-eight, from day to night
But in addition maybe we should park
Upon the terrace at the front, a tank.
Or similar large and armoured vehicle.
It is important that we send a message out
That makes it clear the King's supported well.
Because you're right, indeed, that when we join
The forces we all swear that come what may
We shall protect the King, and so we will.

Enter BUTLER.

BUTLER.
The Leader of the Opposition sir.

CHARLES.
Send him in.

Enter MR STEVENS.

MR STEVENS.
Your Majesty, Sir Gordon, greetings both
I promised to ensure you were updated
On how the House of Commons does respond
Toward the intervention of the King.

CHARLES.
Yes. Well?

MR STEVENS.
It is a mixed bag, of course
There are those on both sides who strongly feel
That we as signed-up members of the House
Did swear we would obey the law as written down
And not, like children, wait until the day
It didn't suit, and then decide in fact
We'd rather not. I'd say that is how we
Conservatives do feel. That we should go
Back to the people and, as you've decreed,
Seek re-election to the House, and then
If we're successful, think about a change.

CHARLES.
Or not.

MR STEVENS.
Or not, precisely right indeed.
Unfortunately those of Labour, and
For what they're worth, the other parties too
Are resolute that we should not dissolve
And should instead in contravention of
The royal decree continue with the House,
And make a legislation that will stop
The King from interference in the State.

Enter CAMILLA.

CHARLES.
Then Mr Stevens take the message back
The King is stubborn and he will not move.
The surest and the smoothest course would be
To make a new election and thereby
We'll ask the people to resolve our spat.

MR STEVENS.
This is what I will press on all of them.
A steady course to chart through rocky seas.

He goes.

SIR GORDON.
Your Majesty, if there's nothing else I will
Go organise the extra troops outside.

CHARLES.
Before you do, there's just one question more.
Despite the nineteenth-century uniform
And strangely soaring bearskin hats they wear,
I wondered if the soldiers' antique guns
Did carry ammunition that was live.

SIR GORDON.
The men that stand so still outside the gates
Do practise with their rifles every week.
The funny hats are just a way to fuzz
The brutal fact the army's on the streets,
And answerable not to the police
Or to the politician's changing whims,
But only to their officer, and so,
By ladder of command, to you, the Crown.
Whatever comes to pass we will be there.

SIR GORDON *goes*.

CAMILLA.
What's all this talk of arms and loaded guns?

CHARLES.
The Parliament refuse to budge an inch,
And like a horde of squatters, occupy
A house that they are not entitled to.

CAMILLA.
But all these people, generals, judges,
Mr Stevens, none of them would be the men
That you in normal circumstance would trust.

CHARLES.
The very air tastes strange these last few days.
But having made a move I now must stick
And see it through, even if I must make
Fair-weather friends, who only seek the sun.

Enter JAMES.

JAMES.
Your Majesty, forgive me bursting in
But news has broken out today: there is
Another problem –

CHARLES.
                    Yes? What problem now?

HARRY *enters with* JESS.

CAMILLA.
Oh Harry! We don't see enough of you.

HARRY.
Camilla, Father, here's my friend, her name
Is Jess, she studies at St Martin's College

CHARLES.
St Martin's College? Good, so you're in art?

JESS.
Yeah

JAMES.
Sir, if I can interrupt –

CHARLES.
Oh yes, James says a crisis looms once more
So good to meet you Jess, but we –

HARRY.
                                    I think
That James's crisis stands within this room.

JAMES.
You are correct.

CHARLES.
                    What do you mean, this room?

HARRY.
Please Dad, if I can be allowed to speak?
For reasons you don't need to understand
A picture made of Jessica that is
Quite intimate has made its way onto
The cover of the London paper and
Will no doubt grace the nationals as well.

There is attack toward her worse than I
Have seen, 'gainst Kate, or me, or Mum, or you,
I think because of class, the public's not
So comfortable with someone like themselves
But let me tell you she is something else
To anything our family has known
I suddenly can see my life before
Was full of stupid idiocy to so
Distract me from a sadness kept within
Distract me cos I had nothing to love,
And although yourself and William are
Most loving in familial ways, I had
No one to share thoughts with, no one who spent
The time to work out who I was, and what
I really needed. She has done all this,
And still does more. A force of nature, makes
Me laugh and think and grow. She's free, so free!
But now she wants to leave me cos of this.

CAMILLA.

I've never heard you speak in such a way
With passion, strength and rhythm too.

CHARLES.

My son has spoken, but the lady's quiet
Please Jessica, come tell me what you think.

JESS.

He's right, that in the last few weeks, we have
Formed a relationship that is unique
I do not want to leave your son, but now
Each hand in London touch on me tonight
I feel such shame it is unbearable.

JAMES.

Sir please, if I can add perspective to
This well-intentioned but ill-fated match –

CHARLES.

I know what you will think dear James.
I need not hear it now.

Beat.

If I defend the freedom of the press
It's with the knowledge they will never live
Up to a higher standard. Naked girls
And boys will illustrate their pages.
Horrific murders will be made still more
Atrocious by intrusion, and they'll make
Hypocrisy an art, insisting that
They stand chief moralist while making cash
As base pornographer. I know this much.
So all that we can do is stand our ground.
For if they're free to print this dirt, then we
Have liberty as well, to answer back.
Dear Jessica, you have done nothing wrong.
I understand the picture causes shame,
And there is little we can do 'bout that.
But Harry is bewitched by you, and though
I once did question what love meant I now
Can see it standing here, so desperate,
Begging you stay. So now you have my word,
You have the royal protection and respect.
Whatever we can do to help we will.
You will be welcome in our family.

JESS.
    But sir that's not –

HARRY.
                    It isn't that we want.

CAMILLA.
    Come Harry, now it's done, your father has
    Been generous with time and inclination.

HARRY.
    I do not want her noble princess made
    Instead descend myself into the mass
    Cast off the princely burden of my birth
    And for my life be Harry, man and friend
    With job, and house, and car and maybe wife.
    I want to go with her into the world
    Not trap her here inside these regal walls.

CAMILLA.
It isn't possible.

HARRY.
If King approves it can through boredom work.
We make no fuss 'cept that I have moved, got job.
And will no longer take the civil list
I'll have no role official and not Prince,
I'll live a life of normalcy, within
This country, rather than atop the mound
Unearned and with a target on my back.

CHARLES.
You would not be a prince?

HARRY.
I'd be your son,
But no, my love for Jessica comes first
Because like you, I don't believe that born
A prince must mean I sacrifice my soul,
My hopes, desires, all that makes me, me.
Instead I should be free to choose my path
We all should! William, yourself, young George
Should be allowed an unpredicted life.

He looks at them.

CHARLES.
You are like opposites, in every way,
But dissimilarity instead does make a match.
So Harry, yes, you may do as you wish.

JAMES.
If I can interrupt, whatever you
May do, this story is distraction when
The throne itself is in dispute. Perhaps
At least postpone this alteration to
When you are safely crowned King

CHARLES.
Alright,
Then after coronation yes?

HARRY.
Okay?

JESS.

Okay.

CHARLES.

And James, in case the press persist
You'll see the lady is defended yes?

JAMES.

…

CHARLES.

You have something to say?

JAMES.

Your Majesty… no.

I'll do as you command.

CHARLES.

Well good. For though my problems are the same
Through Harry's love, I'm driven on again!

They go.

4.3

Kensington.

Enter KATE, *reading the* Evening Standard.

KATE.

It is bewildering that even now
These little rooms of power are stocked full
With white, and southern, likely Oxbridge men.
Without the Queen, the bias is more stark
The King's a man, Prime Minister as well
Combine the front benches of both sides
You'll have a female total of just four.
And so despite emancipation we must look
Towards the harder sex to find the power.
But I know nothing, just a plastic doll
Designed I'm told to stand embodying
A male-created bland and standard wife,
Whose only job is prettying the Prince, and then

If possible, get pregnant with the royal
And noble bump, to there produce an heir.
Or two. And oft I'm told I don't have thought
Or brains to comprehend my strange position.
But being underestimated so
Does give me what these men could never have
Since no one asked me what I think, I can
Observe and plan and learn the way to rule.
For I will be a Queen unlike the ones before
My mother's dad was in the north a miner born
My father came from Leeds, and both of them
When young and inexperienced did risk
Their house and all they had to try and make
A business of their own. But it's not just this stock
I bring to these most distant regal realms
But something more important and precise
I have ambition for my husband yes
And hope my son will grow the finest King
But if I must put up with taunts, and make
So public everything I am, then I
Demand things for myself, I ask no less
Than power to achieve my will in fair
Exchange for total service to the State.
Yes this is what, enthroned, that I will do.
Not simply help my husband in his crown
But wear one of my own.

But here's my husband, he's been on the phone.

Enter WILLIAM.

How did it go?

WILLIAM.
                    I asked him of his plans.

KATE.
    His plans?

WILLIAM.
                    Of what he did intend to do.
Now that there's violent protest up and down
The country 'tween supporters of the Crown
And those who want its swift complete demise.

KATE.
And what said he?

WILLIAM.

        He simply said
The strength of public voice in strong support
Did give him solace that he wasn't wrong.

KATE.
This is an answer clear enough to me.
Charles is stranded, using what's to hand
Does smile and say this was always the plan.

But what he hopes is that from out the blue
There'll grow a noise, a chopping engine sound
And through the clouds a helicopter comes.
And lowering down its harness, scoops him up,
And quickly lifts the tired reckless man
To safety from the bleak and troubled rock.

A BUTLER *enters.*

BUTLER.
Your Highness. The Prime Minister.

WILLIAM.
Prime Minister – I didn't ask him here –

KATE.
I know.

Enter MR EVANS. *Also* SIR MICHAEL, *Head of the Metropolitan Police, in shirt-sleeves.*

Prime Minister –

MR EVANS.

        Duchess, you asked to see
Sir Michael.

KATE.

       You are kind to come attend
On us when you must be distract indeed.

SIR MICHAEL.
Distract is right

KATE.

>   Please tell us latest news

SIR MICHAEL.

>   Last night saw violence spark across the land.
>   In Liverpool, a protest made towards
>   The Mersey, lifting effigy they'd built
>   Based on your father, burnt it bright, then dropped
>   It in the sea. In Oxford marches have
>   Formed on both sides and even as we speak
>   They clash. In Edinburgh, the same, Belfast.
>   In Norfolk one poor man was pushed through glass
>   And now does lie in most intensive care.
>   But London is the worst –

KATE.

>   The worst?

SIR MICHAEL.

>   We are
>   Your Highness, much too stretched.

WILLIAM.

>   Then find reserves
>   To flood the streets.

SIR MICHAEL.

>   Reserves are out. No more
>   To come. We'll maybe last another day.

Beat.

KATE.

>   Then we should let you carry on. Our thanks.

SIR MICHAEL *goes.*

MR EVANS.

>   The Speaker will not open up the House
>   Because he fears it is illegal as things stand.
>   And so the Members of the Parliament
>   Do sit, just as four hundred years ago
>   In Westminster Hall instead. But because
>   We've only half the House, we can't make laws

WILLIAM.
>We should stay calm, for still you are in charge.
>This is the way it works until there's new
>Prime Minister, the old fulfils the task.

MR EVANS.
>Already Mr Stevens has questioned
>My right to make decisions.

WILLIAM.
>   Services
>Are functioning well, the schools, transport, health?

MR EVANS.
>No sir, the schools have closed, doctors are stretched.
>The bloodshed worsens every day we wait
>And while we in the House attempt to calm
>The King has generals round to tea, and parks
>A tank in Buckingham Palace grounds.
>Perhaps exaggeration but there is talk
>Of civil war.

WILLIAM.
>   A joke.

MR EVANS.
>   It's not at all.

KATE.
>The British stock, which was considered safe
>Has in two whole weeks completely crashed.

WILLIAM.
>Prime Minister, in private, I, of course,
>Wholeheartedly do give my full support.
>But this is for the Parliament to solve

KATE.
>Oh William, they can't! Parliament is impotent.
>And just become a meeting house of men.
>The time has come to go and halt this mess.

MR EVANS.
>Your Highness, please, your wife is quite correct.

WILLIAM.
I can't.

KATE.
For George!

WILLIAM.
You must not make me.

MR EVANS.
Then sir I think you will be Prince no more
And none that follow will be King again.

Pause.

WILLIAM.
You are a man of serious intent.
Throughout our recent troubles you have shown
My father great respect and courtesy.

Beat.

Prime Minister go back to Number Ten
You can leave it to me. I'll bring an end
To this unnecessary episode.

MR EVANS.
I thank you sir. An intervention's what
We need.

MR EVANS, *and party, leave.*

WILLIAM.
You set me up.

KATE.
I lifted you, my one.
To where by right of birth you ought to be.

He looks at her a moment.

WILLIAM.
Then if it's done, it's done at once.

ATTENDANTS *go.*

KATE.
But husband wait. I know the way.

WILLIAM.

The way?

KATE.
We're told the world's a play of surfaces
Where meaning's made through only what is shown
You must then focus 'pon the public eye
You dress your best. And so, of course, shall I.

She goes.

WILLIAM *follows.*

4.4.

Enter JAMES *and a* TELEVISION PRODUCER.

TELEVISION PRODUCER.
And so we thought this room might serve us well.
A neutral colour, good acoustic and
The space to house the country's journalists.

JAMES.
Not just the country, all across the world
The people wait to hear directly from the King.

TELEVISION PRODUCER.
Of course, that's true.

A pause.

JAMES.
Would you be one of them?

TELEVISION PRODUCER.

You mean a king?

JAMES.
I mean a man or woman standing there
In front of camera's gaze, instead of you
Or I, who seek to do the best we can
While hidden from the public's view.

TELEVISION PRODUCER.
>This may seem strange, but sometimes I wake up
>From nightmares where I have been on TV
>And something's happened, just by chance, perhaps
>A light has blown, or chair collapsed, but I
>Am shocked, and jumping look ridiculous.
>And then that clip goes viral and from then
>Forever more, I am the girl who jumped
>It is the matter of my life, and when
>I die it will be what is writ, not all
>I did, and wanted, and achieved, but that:
>A captured idiocy stuck on repeat.

Enter CHARLES.

>Your Majesty. Welcome. Here's the microphone
>Into which you'll speak, the autocue is there

CHARLES.
>It's good. Thank you. How long do we now have?

TELEVISION PRODUCER.
>Perhaps we'll let them in, in oh, five mins?

JAMES.
>In that case let us have a moment to prepare?

TELEVISION PRODUCER.
>Of course, I'll be next door, just let me know.

The TELEVISION PRODUCER *goes.*

CHARLES.
>I'm still not full persuaded of the need
>To speak like this.

JAMES.
>   Every night,
>Prime Minister, and politicians of all creeds,
>With nothing else to do, now that their normal
>Auditorium is shut down,
>Do hop to television, and once there
>They make the case in detail, all the time
>Against Your Majesty. My fear is that

Without your voice in contest heard
The public mood will turn away. And so
Although I know it's your idea of hell.
You must here stand, and meet the press.

CHARLES *stands in the right place*.

Remember that they are, near to a man
Surprised that you have leapt to their defence.
And thus will be most generous to your views.

CHARLES.
I hope that's right, we've never been that close.

Enter WILLIAM, *with* KATE.

But William, what's this? I didn't know
You would be here, I thought you disapproved.

WILLIAM.
I'll always serve the interests of the Crown.

KATE.
As family, we should be seen as one.
James says it's what they will expect of us.

CHARLES.
So it was James persuaded you to come?

WILLIAM.
It was in conversation yes, we thought
It would be best to come along like this.
How are the arrangements James, you spoke about?

JAMES.
As often with TV, a scrabbled mess
But all should be sufficient for our needs.

CHARLES.
I don't know how to thank you James.
It will be now with pride and strength of clan
I stand my ground and state my case.

WILLIAM.
We'll stand indeed.

The TELEVISION PRODUCER *enters*.

TELEVISION PRODUCER.
                    Your Highness, Duchess.
    Yes, ma'am you will be standing there, and sir,
    Just to the right hand of His Majesty.

CHARLES.
    As always James you've foreseen everything.
    The picture here, like this, is now complete.
    The family will be my backdrop and the news
    Will say, the country's safe, and clear united.

TELEVISION PRODUCER.
    So are we ready now?

CHARLES.
                    We are, proceed.

TELEVISION PRODUCER.
    Okay then, hurry up!

    CHARLES *stands. The* TELEVISION PRODUCER *opens
    the door and in floods the* PRESS, *to find* CHARLES *waiting
    for them.*

CHARLES.
    Good afternoon, I'll give you all some time
    To get arranged I know you like to barge
    And jostle for position. Hi Nick! And… John.

TELEVISION PRODUCER.
    We'll make a start in sixty seconds' time
    Is everyone arranged where they can see?
    That's good, so thirty, twenty, ten…

    CHARLES *goes to move forward, when suddenly –*
    WILLIAM *walks quickly in front of him, to the podium.*

    CHARLES, *confused, stands to the side.* JAMES *tries to
    guide him to a chair, but he refuses.*

    Live in five, four…

    Bright light – on WILLIAM. CHARLES *to the side, behind
    him, in full view.*

WILLIAM.

> Good afternoon. And gosh, there's quite a few
> Of you.

A laugh.

> So thank you all for coming here today,
> And for the people listening in at home,
> Across the country and the Commonwealth.
> My wife and I have been so shocked
> By scenes unfolding, here and overseas.
> My father has, through noble conscience said,
> As is his right, he will withhold assent,
> And furthermore, as is legal too,
> He has dismissed elected Government.
> Of course this has resulted in disquiet
> Not just in homes and streets, or in the House,
> But in our family too. My wife and I
> Respect my father's choices, but, do wish,
> It could have been avoided. And so.
> Today I do announce that I, as Prince
> Of Wales, from now will try to mediate
> Between the King and House of Commons.
> I'm convinced there is a way to move on this.
> Without the need for further violence, and
> Respecting both democracy and the
> Ancient British power of anointed King.

> I have my father's blessing in this role.
> He is as keen as I to see an end
> To this destructive and divisive time.
> I'm also lucky to have Catherine too.
> For all of this was actually her idea.
> Turns out she's cleverer than all of us!

Some laughter.

> She'll sort us out!

More laughter.

CHARLES *turns to face* WILLIAM.

Looks at him for a moment. Furious.

A camera flash, then CHARLES *turns, walks off the platform and out of the door.*

Flashing of photographs.

My father's finding this quite difficult.
As you'd imagine, so he needs support.
Forgive me if I don't take questions now
But once we're up and running, I will speak
Again. Perhaps we'll just do photographs?
Thank you, thank you Nick, and John.

He stands back and smiles. KATE *joins him.*

Photos are taken of the family – shouting – adulation.

ACT FIVE

5.1

Buckingham Palace.

The sound of the crowd outside.

CHARLES *enters with a book.*

CHARLES.
    I have been through the archive many times
    But read as King each word seems made afresh.
    I have been seeking moments which relate
    Precisely to the current state of play
    Our English law is based on precedent
    And when I'm called to make my case I must
    Have all the facts to hand, examples of
    When monarchs in the past have also done
    The same as I, or very near. And so.
    Here's Walter Bagehot, eighteen sixty-seven,
    Explaining changes to balance of
    The Crown and State. I read it as a child.
    One line stands out: Bagehot explains that now
    The monarch's mostly ceremonial
    And only can expect, from hereon in:
    The right to be consulted (which I've not)
    The right to encourage (which is all I do),
    And most importantly the right to warn.
    'The Right to Warn' so warning is the thing
    It's only what I do, I warn, but even that
    I'm told's too much and so must tolerate
    This constant fuzz of bright white noise
    That emanates from out the mob.

The sound of the crowd continues.

The BUTLER *enters.*

BUTLER.
    Your Majesty.

CHARLES.
Roberts?

BUTLER.
James Reiss waits outside.

CHARLES.
The traitor's at the gate. What does he want?

BUTLER.
To see you sir. He'll say no more than that.

CHARLES.
Allow him in.

The BUTLER *goes. Enter* JAMES.

The silver lining when someone defects
Is you don't have to see them any more.

JAMES.
I wanted to explain.

CHARLES.
You knew what William would say to them?

JAMES.
Indeed I made it possible for him to speak.

CHARLES.
You ambushed me.

JAMES.
                    It was, just as he said,
The Duchess's idea. And William, knowing
Not just that I desired the bill
Against the press to pass, but that I thought
Your current course of action fatal to
The strong continued influence of the Crown,
Did suggest this plan, which although I knew
Would cause you pain, I did believe would when
It all was weighed, be thought of as the best.

CHARLES.
It matters not. It will not work. For I
Am not in need of mediation here.

There is no common ground, no compromise.
Anointed not by man, but God, I don't
Negotiate but issue my commands.
So here I'll sit, and wait for what I want
To come into existence. I can wait,
A very long time, I have my books to read.

JAMES.

But sir, you must –

CHARLES.

You're surely not intending still to work,
For me, not after treachery like this?

JAMES.

Your son has offered me employment.

CHARLES.

So leave. You've said your bit. And no, before
You ask, you're not forgiven. Actually
I hope you fail in everything you do.

JAMES.

Then sir, farewell.

He goes.

A roar from the crowd outside.

CHARLES *goes to the window.*

CHARLES.

Be calmed! Your King commands you now to cease!
And yet they do not hear, another case
Of this, the disproportion of the features.
When unlike me, their ears, so rarely used
Are shrivelled up and tiny, but their mouth
From making constant noise, is swollen up
And when not talking fixes in a grin
Of no emotion, Botoxed into place.
Be quiet all! Some silence here! But no.
Although they say it's anger on the news
They danced around a fire lit within
The fountain and seemed happy there last night.
But wait, there's movement, noise, a grinding sound

The tank below, its engines started up
It's moving round, what's happening now?
The tank was there for show, it should not act
And I should be aware of any change
And yet – it doesn't move towards the crowd
Instead it's off the other way, and out of sight.
I should be told if things have changed, Roberts!

Roberts! Where is that man – some butler he, who's
never here!

WILLIAM *enters*.

William – Where's Roberts gone?

WILLIAM.
I said to take an hour off.

CHARLES.

You said –

WILLIAM.
That's right Your Majesty we need to speak.

CHARLES.
'Your Majesty'? But William, it's me.
Despite the horrid things you've done, it's me.
So call me Dad, or Father if you like,
But not Your Majesty, like all the rest.

WILLIAM.
I call you that for that is what you are
Before my father, long before all else
You are the King, and that's to whom I speak.

Pause.

CHARLES.
But William come look at this, a book
It's Bagehot from the ancient archive here
It does enlighten on the changing way
The monarchy has influence over
The State. It is a thing of quiet beauty.

I'm like a book myself, stuck on the shelf
For years, ignored and waiting, only judged

By one small sliver of the cover whole,
And sitting thus unopened and unused,
The outer surface gathers dust and fades
But if the moment comes to read the tome,
And it's removed and rarely opened up
The words and thoughts inside are here
As fresh and potent as the day of print.

WILLIAM.
What did he write?

CHARLES.
     That I can warn the State
And more expect to fairly be consulted

WILLIAM.
They did at length consult the Queen before –

CHARLES.
My mother's dead, and we must start again.

WILLIAM.
You think too much on books and history.

CHARLES.
But what is power held if never used?

WILLIAM.
Our duty's not to simply sit indoors
And hope it is resolved, but to engage
All parties and attempt to find a way –

CHARLES.
'Engage all parties'? King's no such duty

WILLIAM.
A duty royal. That's shared amongst us all.

CHARLES.
I will speak harshly William that I
Do not request your counsel, I do not need
Another view. Instead it is support
Expected and support that you must give.
I know that at your age you'll have a sense
That in the prime of life, you shouldn't be
Attending on an old and feeble parent,

So there's temptation then to patronise
Ironically the ones who gave you birth,
To roll your eyes, and make a joke about
The modern things they do not understand.
But doing this is seen by all around
As juvenile, the mockery of age
As easy humour, and actually it's wise
To listen well, respect those older, and
Most subtly to learn and grow beside
To draw upon their strength while standing close
And offering support to deal with age.

WILLIAM.
It's not about a father and a son
It is the title I address today
And not my father who of course I love

CHARLES.
You cannot make distinction 'tween the two
When both of us are born and grown towards
A single purpose from our opening breath
To final gasp, our whole existence, all
Relationships and yes our family,
Is every atom crowned and every cell
Within our bodies built by monarchy.

Your action yesterday was infantile
And does not alter anything at all.
You should apologise for such betrayal.
But I will put it down to youth, and nerves.

Now help me and go fetch good Roberts here.
The tank is still remiss, and all those guards
Sir Gordon kindly put in place have gone.

WILLIAM.
I know.

CHARLES.
                You know? What do you mean you know?

WILLIAM.
Sir Gordon came to Kensington. We spoke.
I said with the unrest and violence that
Has spread across the country we should not

Be stoking it with these provocative
Militaristic shows.

CHARLES.

And what said he?

WILLIAM.

That it was not a show and swore he had
In consultation here with you agreed
It was important that the Palace is
Defended from attacks within the crowd.

CHARLES.

Exactly, you should not have questioned it.

WILLIAM.

But having heard his answer I went on
That in an hour I would head towards
The Palace in the car, the same I drove
That sunny day I married my fair wife.
Escorted by police I'll drive straight down
The Mall and enter through the guarded gates.
I then intend to go around the yard
And if, I said, there is a tank, I'll ask
My men in blue that they do move it off.
Because it is a danger, having such
A deadly weapon aimed towards the crowd.
Sir Gordon stared, he stopped and thought.
And then he asked if I was really serious?
Would I incite a clash between the troops
Who all held guns and the unarmed police?
I stared at him, just as I stare at you,
And said I'm looking forward to my drive.

Beat.

And when as promised I drove down the Mall
Police on either side, expecting that
The crowd would see me and attack the car,
Instead they saw who steered and parted there
To let us through, and as we went between,
The mob, a silence fell upon them all.
It was most strange, they stopped and watched us go.

Beat.

There was no tank, or military might.
And just two guards stood to attention there.

Beat.

And as the gates began to close, one girl
Called out 'You tell him Will' and so I must.

CHARLES.
Must tell me what?

WILLIAM.
You can't go back from your decision now.

CHARLES.
Agreed, retreating now would be the end.

WILLIAM.
And yet you can't progress, the Parliament
Will never hold elections as you wish.

CHARLES.
We'll see.

WILLIAM.
So I propose on coronation day,
We have two thrones upon the dais placed,
And sat on cushions next to them are
Two crowns awaiting royal heads to rest.

CHARLES.
Two thrones, two crowns, it is not possible
For Britain and the Commonwealth to have
As you suggest two kings in tandem rule.

WILLIAM.
No not two kings. A King and Queen.

CHARLES.
You mean Camilla, oft we have discussed –

WILLIAM.
Camilla no.

CHARLES.
                    Then what do you intend?

WILLIAM.

…

CHARLES.

Cos if it's what I think then you must speak
The words of treachery yourself and shank
Your father with a full and clear betrayal.

WILLIAM.

I mean myself and Kate are crowned instead.

Beat.

CHARLES.

And what of me? I simply stand aside?

WILLIAM.

You offer abdication and explain
Since taking on the role, you've felt your age.

Pause.

CHARLES.

There's something in your face I recognise
A stern expression, reckless and so bold,
It was Diana where I saw it last,
And I had hoped that it had died with her.
But here it is, in you, ambition lurks.

WILLIAM.

I'm proud of that ambition, proud of her
Who plucked so young before she knew the world
And thrust into a den of lions, keen
For meat, was given no protection, and
When you decided to make return to one
You always loved, you threw my mum aside
Discarded and destroyed her by repute

CHARLES.

I loved your mother at the time and did
My very best to make sure you weren't harmed

WILLIAM.

And that will be your tombstone – 'Did my best.
At least I tried!' A plea for effort rather than effect.

That's you as husband, you as son, as father too.
And now as King. But all our sympathy
Is withered up and dry. This is a job.
You should have got it right and you did not.

CHARLES.
Be careful what you say, you've always had
My unconditional and total love
I said whatever thing you did, my love
Would never end, but with those words my mind
Does change. I think that I could wash my hands
Of you and not look back.

WILLIAM.
                              Unneeded and
Romantic gestures seem to be your fault.
You needn't let me go. There doesn't have
To be this constant turbulence you've brought.
I will as King return to what your mother did,
Stability and certainty, above all else.

CHARLES.
I will not abdicate! Ungrateful boy!
I'll never give away the crown, for me
It's duty and my calling, things to do!
I know, don't ask me how, that I will be
The greatest King of all.

WILLIAM.
The greatest King? And so you shall.
For when they write the history books 'bout this
They will tell stories crisis-like about
The stormy days after the Queen had died
And how for weeks you contemplated hard
Upon the right and proper thing to do,
And in the end decided for the good of all,
Your people and their long-term happiness
You'd selflessly stand down and pass it on,
To younger hands, more popular and with
More time to reign. This move will then be seen,
Today and ever more, as when the Crown
Did save itself and through a clever choice

An idea of the greatest King we had,
Renewed the brand to last another century.

CHARLES.
A nice conceit, but no, I will be King
As ruler not as doormat stepped across.

WILLIAM *goes to the door.*

WILLIAM.
Mr Evans.

MR EVANS *enters.*

CHARLES.
No go! I do not wish to see you now.

MR EVANS.
Your Majesty, this is a sorry day
But if you cannot sign the law you must
Make way for one who can. Your good repute
Will be preserved, and monarchy survive.
I have brought here, a document to make
Official abdication, so we can
Achieve a common goal: Stability.

CHARLES.
Who made this thing, this paper here?

MR EVANS.
The Civil Service drew it up today.

CHARLES.
And printed out in haste, there are mistakes
In spelling.

WILLIAM.
Will you sign?

CHARLES.
I will not.

CAMILLA *enters. Behind her, following, is* KATE
and HARRY.

CAMILLA.
Is it true?

CHARLES.
>It is.

CAMILLA turns and slaps WILLIAM. CHARLES
meanwhile stares at HARRY.

CAMILLA.
>A vile and nasty child.
And what's that document you're holding there?
You must do nothing till we have consulted
With experts on the constitution and
The lawyers that we pay so much money to.

She looks at it.

I thought it Harry who was wild, but you
Have now by far surpassed his worst excess

Charles would not sign the bill, he will not this.
I realise you and Catherine are the King
And Queen of column inches but you're just
A Duke and Duchess here. The King is King.
He will not sign. Now both of you away.

KATE.
Your thin opinion of us demonstrates
How out of touch you are, and jealous too.
Our looks don't make us cruel, our youth is not
An ignorance, and detail in the way we dress
Should not be thought as vanity, but is
Part of the substance only we provide.
We know the world. Our column inches are
The greatest influence that we possess.
Majesty, sign. And bring an end to this

CHARLES goes to HARRY.

CHARLES.
My son, your loyalty!
For your relationship with Jessica,
Has been a burning light these darkest days.

HARRY.
The people turn to William. This is
The only way. I am convinced.

Beat.

CHARLES.
Harry. Please.

My boys. My little boys.

Pause.

Of course you're scared. But I know what I do.
So sit. Let's talk. If Roberts's gone I will
Myself go fetch some tea, and someone here
Will show me how it's made. That was a joke.

HARRY.
We'll have the tea, and sit and be your sons
But first you abdicate

CHARLES.
                    And if I don't?

WILLIAM.
Then we will leave, and wait, and not return
Yes, us, and Kate, the children. Family all.
This is tough love, we're all agreed it's best.
You will not see us till you change your mind.

Pause.

CHARLES.
I will not see my sons? My grandchildren too?

Pause.

I cannot live alone.

CAMILLA.
                    You're not alone
And even if you were, well better that
Than father-servant to your shallow sons.
The man I married will not bend, or break
Instead, as all the world throws rotten fruit
He will be firm and tie his life onto
The stake of principle.

Pause.

You boys should go, and take this spiteful drip.
He is not worthy of the office that he has.

CHARLES.
I cannot live alone.

They all look at him.

The greatest King?

A pause.

He signs.

So there, it's done, the King is at an end.
I will retreat to bed, and when I wake
To a new dawn, I'll simply be an old
Forgotten gardener, who potters round
And talks to plants and chuckles to himself.
Whilst far away the King and Queen do rule
Over a golden age of monarchy,
That bothers no one, does no good, and is
A pretty plastic picture with no meaning.

He goes.

CAMILLA *looks at* WILLIAM. *Then follows.*

5.2

Westminster Abbey.

Before the coronation.

To one side, CHARLES *and* CAMILLA *wait.* CHARLES *is
unreadable – watching over the preamble…just watching…*

MR STEVENS *enters and goes to* CHARLES.

MR STEVENS.
Your Majesty, may I personally say that I
Despite my public view of happiness
In fact do think this tragic, and a hard

And bitter end to what you tried to do.
I'll always think of Charles as noble King
As man of honour much too principled
For realpolitik. You may be gone
In constitution but to me you will
Remain my king of hearts, of all before
You are the very best we never had.

An awkward pause. CHARLES *doesn't look at him.*

He smiles and moves on to his place.

Enter MR EVANS. *He sees* CHARLES *and decides not to have a conversation. Instead he walks on to his place.*

Next, JESS *enters. In contrast to everyone else, she's wearing smart jeans and a relatively normal top. She's holding the seating plan, but is confused.*

COOTSY *enters. He sees* JESS, *unsure of herself.*

COOTSY.
    Ah. Jessica. Didn't fancy dressing up?

JESS.
    No.

COOTSY.
    Couldn't afford it?

He goes. Enter JAMES.

JAMES.
    Miss Jessica, why do you seem so lost,
    And stand unoriented in the Abbey aisle?

JESS.
    I'll not tell you, you have no love for me.
    The King said help but now it's even worse
    There's every picture from my wayward youth
    Made weekly fodder for the *Daily Mail*,
    And any minor misdemeanour makes
    A banner headline in the *Sun*. From how
    They write of what I do, you'd think that art
    Was rated worse than brutal homicide.

JAMES.

Well miss, I'm not sure how much art you've seen,
But it can often feel like one has died.

JESS.

I understood the law was changed for this
When journalism turns to voyeurs' gawp.

JAMES.

Indeed but somehow nothing has been done.

JESS.

Because you want me gone.

JAMES.

Not true, I've tried my best to help.
These stories do us both no good at all.

JESS.

Your eyes are small, I don't know what to think.

JAMES.

Tell me what's your problem miss.

JESS.

The seating plan, my name does not appear.

JAMES.

Well let me see.

He looks.

It's true there is no Jessica. You're sure
The Prince did make his invitation known?

JESS.

I'm sure.

Enter HARRY.

JAMES.

Perhaps it would be best,
To find out from the man himself, for here
He comes, so handsome in his uniform.
Your Highness, yes, it's such a happy day.
Although I wouldn't know it from your pale
And cloudy face. Here's Jessica who seems

Omitted from the seating plan. Maybe
You'll know a little more 'bout this than I.

He goes.

JESS.

Okay, so where am I supposed to sit?
Not next to you, it seems, not even near.
In fact I am not found at all. Are you
Alright? I've never seen you grey and stark.

HARRY.

You'll not attend today, as William
And Kate are crowned, you'll have to watch outside.

JESS.

Outside? But why?

HARRY.

I...

JESS.

Harry?

HARRY.

My brother, talking with his wife, and close
Advisers, bearing all the photographs
And stories of your past that do appear,
In mind. Do feel it would be best you not
Attend. You are too big a risk to what
He needs: Stability –

JESS.

But that's –

HARRY.

And furthermore
He's asked me personally if I would stop
All contact with you and resume the way
I was before, a singleton, amusing
Mostly, clownish and unthreatening.
Therefore I'm sat, as previously planned
With Cootsy, Spencer. These most harmless friends.

JESS.

I hope you quickly told him where to go.

HARRY.
He is my brother.

JESS.
Are you fucking joking?

HARRY.
But more than that, he's now anointed King.

Pause.

JESS.
So King can tell you what to feel and who
You love. The King's dictator of your heart.

HARRY.
My heart was made by King, if I betray
Allegiance then the little that I am is gone.

JESS.
But things have changed. He has to understand
And if you loved me you'd fight this.

Beat.

Or if I have to go, you'd come with me.

HARRY.
I want to.

Pause. Then he stands to attention, looks away.

It's starting soon.

She stares at him for a moment. Then goes.

HARRY *stands alone.*

Music starts and he takes his place.

A choir begins singing, and orchestra plays.

All stand.

The doors open and KATE *enters with* ATTENDANTS.

She processes in and sits on the throne.

The procession of WILLIAM *enters with* ATTENDANTS.

Once settled, the ARCHBISHOP OF CANTERBURY *comes forward.*

ARCHBISHOP OF CANTERBURY.
I here present to you King William your undoubted King.
Wherefore all you who are come this day to do your homage
and service.

Is Your Majesty willing to take the Oath?

WILLIAM.
I am willing.

ARCHBISHOP OF CANTERBURY.
Will you solemnly promise and swear to govern the Peoples
of the United Kingdom of Great Britain and Northern
Ireland, Canada, Australia, New Zealand, and of your
Possessions and other Territories to any of them belonging or
pertaining, according to their respective laws and customs?

WILLIAM.
I solemnly promise so to do.

ARCHBISHOP OF CANTERBURY.
Will you to your power cause Law and Justice, in Mercy, to
be executed in all your judgements?

WILLIAM.
I will.

ARCHBISHOP OF CANTERBURY.
Will you to the utmost of your power maintain the Laws of
God and the true profession of the Gospel?

Will you maintain and preserve inviolably the settlement of
the Church of England, and the doctrine, worship, discipline,
and government thereof, as by law established in England?

WILLIAM.
All this I promise to do.

A choir sings.

The ARCHBISHOP *goes and gets the crown.*

He brings it forward to WILLIAM.

CHARLES *suddenly stands – a consternation. This isn't supposed to happen.*

He goes and looks at the crown.

The choir stops singing.

CHARLES *reaches for the crown. The* ARCHBISHOP *is unsure.*

Glances at WILLIAM. *Then gives the crown to* CHARLES.

A moment.

CHARLES.
It is much heavier than I thought.

He looks at WILLIAM.

A moment.

And from the side, bejewelled, it looks so rich
But turn it thus, and this is what you see

Nothing.

Beat.

My son. God save you.

CHARLES *puts the crown on* WILLIAM*'s head.*

CHARLES *slowly collapses and sits on the step.* WILLIAM *stands.*

A long pause.

WILLIAM *looks to the* ARCHBISHOP.

ARCHBISHOP OF CANTERBURY.
God save the King!

ALL.
God save the King!

End.

www.nickhernbooks.co.uk

 facebook.com/nickhernbooks

twitter.com/nickhernbooks